Biomechanics
for the Equestrian
MOVE WELL TO RIDE WELL

Biomechanics
for the Equestrian
MOVE WELL TO RIDE WELL

Debbie Rolmanis

JA Allen

First published in 2019 by
by JA Allen

JA Allen is an imprint of
The Crowood Press Ltd
Ramsbury, Marlborough
Wiltshire SN8 2HR

www.crowood.com

British Library Cataloguing-in-Publication Data
A catalogue record for this book is available from the British Library.

ISBN 978 1 908809 84 1

Diagrams by Carole Vincer

Disclaimer
The author and publisher do not accept responsibility in any manner
whatsoever for any error or omission, or any loss, damage, injury, adverse
outcome, or liability of any kind incurred as a result of the use of any of the
information contained in this book, or reliance upon it.

Typeset by Jean Cussons Typesetting, Diss, Norfolk

Printed and bound in India by Replika Press Pvt Ltd

Contents

Introduction

Who wants to ride better? Who wants to move with less pain? Who wants to avoid a hip replacement? And who wants age to not be a barrier to all the things you love doing? Me! I want all those things! That is what I decided a few years ago and, working with riders of all levels, across a multitude of disciplines, I knew that these were things they wanted too.

I haven't always been interested in how the body works. I was a sporty kid; not the worst on the court or in the pool or on a horse, but certainly not the best either. I didn't think twice about not being able to do things until I was thirteen and receiving physiotherapy for a broken collar bone (yes, I did fall off a horse) when I was diagnosed with congenital scoliosis. Apparently a couple of my vertebrae were 'incomplete', which had forced my spine to make the shape of a winding mountain road as opposed to the normal column that really would be preferable. For the first time I was made very aware of my body, especially on my one and only visit to the specialist who announced that I should never again get on a horse. Although I ignored him, it did awaken a curiosity in me and over the next few years I sought help from 'alternative' therapies; I stuck with the ones who told me what I wanted to hear and continued my riding career. Subsequently I became a personal trainer; understanding how the body worked not only helped me to coach riders, but also to keep myself strong and mobile. By this point my interest in all things performance was well and truly entrenched and I went on to become a sports therapist for horse and rider to help unravel some body and performance issues.

I worked with riding clients of all levels, ages, shapes and sizes for over a decade, and patterns of dysfunctions – common themes of pain, positional frustrations and horse training 'trouble' – appeared across the board. Elite riders would show up with the same physical niggles as amateurs and, although improvements were being made, niggling and insidious issues would continue. I knew I was missing something. Seemingly fit, active people were suffering with pain and dysfunction, which was impacting them both on the ground and in the saddle. The gap in my knowledge was understanding the body's non-negotiable, indelible need for movement – not movement in terms of a workout at the gym or a thirty-minute run, but consistent, varied, aligned movement of the entire body. The work I was doing was facilitating the opportunity for good movement, but the missing link was the actual good movement. As soon as a rider left my clinic, they would continue to move their bodies in the same way as they had on their way in. Little wonder their problems were recurring. The way the rider moved during their everyday life was impacting their body in the most significant way, and when I realized this, I noticed *every* rider I work with suffering with similar patterns.

Delving into the world of biomechanics, discovering how loads shape our bodies and how our bodies are designed to thrive from movement, has turned my practice on its head. It is now less about treatment and more about movement education. There is nothing more powerful than corrective movement done all of the time. Real change is only possible if the body is moved how it was designed to be moved, and it isn't about carving time out of your day to do it. Every rider I work with is time poor, so trying to stick to an exercise regime or time at the gym is often not practical and, as will become clear, is not necessarily the best for the body. Classes once a week can be really useful, but they can also present challenges to the body if it is turning up with muscle imbalances, immobility and vulnerable joints. Bringing a stable foundation to the exercise you want to do will give you greater results and provide you with more of a safeguard against injury.

Riding is complicated: we all know that, and every rider I know just wants to be better at it and keep their horse sound. The truth is that the body you bring to the saddle plays a massive role in dictating your riding journey. Everything you do in the saddle – how you sit and where you sit – will influence the way the horse loads his limbs, his back, his pelvis and his forehand. Adjusting your position in the saddle is fine for small tweaks, but the shape your body is in on the ground will be the same shape it will be in on the horse. That is to say, if you have a sore back, a stuck hip

and a frozen shoulder on the ground, these will impact everything you do in the saddle and will dictate how your horse has to move. Knowing how to move yourself away from pain and dysfunction on the ground will change how you sit in the saddle; riding well doesn't just happen in the hours you spend riding: it happens in the way you walk the dog, pick out feet and drive the car. Nobody has a 'perfect' body (just ask them), yet we all only get one for the duration of our life and we live in it all the time! Your body carries with it your past, present and future. As you will see, your ancestors left you with a blueprint of an exceptional machine and this book will help you unearth the body you probably never knew you had. The present shape of your body is different from what it once was. It is constantly in flow, which means you also have the power to control how your shape will change in the future. Educating yourself about your body is one of the greatest gifts you can give yourself and it is my intention with this book to give you the knowledge you need to love the body you are living in, both in and out of the saddle. This is the book that is going to show you how to move well to ride well.

Part 1

Your Movement Story

If you spend any time at all thinking about the human body, from what you see to what lies beneath your skin, chances are you will consider it as a collection of parts – organs, tissues, systems and limbs that operate independently from each other and which largely perform tasks without a whole lot of input from you. However, if that were the case there probably wouldn't be a need for this book. The reality is your body responds to everything you provide it with, and it also responds to everything you don't provide it with in terms of nutrition, hydration, emotional well-being (stress, fear, anger) and movement. As an adult, you will be well versed with the basic needs of a human body: good nutrition from a healthy and well-balanced diet, sufficient daily hydration from clean, plain water (0.033ml for every kg of bodyweight if you weren't sure) and most of you are probably all too aware of how stress doesn't always serve your body positively. What is rarely touted as a life-giving essential is the basic human need for movement. You might know you need to exercise, yes, but the prescribed hour a day at the gym, or a thirty-minute run, or a class once a week, or riding your horse (although better than not moving at all) is only one tiny chapter of your movement story; it's similar to knowing you should eat your greens, but greens alone do not make a complete diet.

The modern exercise prescription is not a complete movement diet for the body and to understand why it's not enough, it's time to look at the physiology of movement.

1 The Physiology of Movement

Movement relates to the positions you have your body in all of the time. How your body is organized determines how it copes with the loads that are placed upon it and therefore what shape the tissues of the body are in. You are loading your body all of the time, which means you are shaping your body all of the time; whether you are sitting down or climbing a mountain, your body is receiving and responding to loads like a lump of clay being moulded into a shape. The form that you create depends on the way you move, how often you move and how differently you move. The shape of your body today, from the position of your spine to the direction your feet point, tells its very own movement story and, as a rider, this is the story your horse will read when you get in the saddle. So, how is it that your shape is dictated by movement? To understand how to create a shape that serves you, it is first necessary to take a look at cells.

CELLS

Your body is a matrix of cells. Every tissue and organ in the body is made of cells. They run in your blood, they form skin and hair, they make and destroy bone, they build and deplete muscle mass, they fight disease, and they help to organize the body in time and space. They are everywhere, all of the time, and they are all connected to one another via a supportive and behaviour-regulating scaffolding known as the extra-cellular matrix. This means that whenever you move a limb or change the configuration of your body parts, you are also adjusting the arrangement of your cells. This cell influence is happening all of the time because of loads. From how you hold a pen to how you sit on a horse, to the loads created by the tension of your waistband, you are constantly providing input to some area of your body. Nothing goes unnoticed and every movement has a reaction. The movements you make (and don't make) are quite literally shaping your body.

EXTRA-CELLULAR MATRIX

The extra-cellular matrix is made up of proteins and polysaccharides (carbohydrates). Its function is to bind cells together and regulate a number of cellular activities.

The effect of load on cells

Loading is the process by which cells receive, sense and translate physical forces and express these loads as your unique human form; from the shape of your bones to the length of your muscles, cells control it all. The body evolved to thrive on movement, and this is confirmed via cell behaviour. Cells require a consistent (and fairly constant) amount of squashing, bending and general deformation of shape not only to stay healthy, but to stay alive. Without any mechanical input or use, even with the best nutrition, cells will not survive. How this shows up in real terms is seen in your posture, your bone density, your muscle mass and the location of your muscle mass. The shape of your body today tells a story not only about what you have been feeding it, but also how you have been loading your cells.

Your body is receiving mechanical stimulation all day, every day. It receives it if you are sitting down, standing, riding, walking or grooming. Your cells are affected differently depending on the shoes you are standing in, right through to whether your trousers are a little snug around the waistband. If you sit down all day your body will adjust differently than if you were standing or walking all day. If you ride eight horses each day, the shape of your cells and the cells you utilize will be different from those of someone who has never sat on a horse, and if you ride after some time off you will certainly know all the new cells you have loaded the next day!

When you think about loads, it is also necessary to consider loads that impact all of your senses. Sensory organs receive loads via pressure (for example, eyes), skin receives loads via touch through clothing and shoes (with new loads experienced as blisters) and your musculo-skeletal system is constantly dealing with the loads imposed by gravity.

The human body is multi-dimensional, meaning that it is made from a range of parts that all contribute to how it functions as a whole. Each joint and soft tissue requires specific movements to keep them healthy, and this can only be achieved if the body is moved in a variety of different ways on a regular basis. It is the variety that ensures that all the cells of the body receive some mechanical input so that they stay alive. Problems, such as pain and lack of mobility, occur when your movements all use the same mechanics and therefore only target the same cells. Walking the same way and carrying things the same way, all the way through to always brushing your teeth with the same

hand, will squash and bend some cells and leave others untouched. This imbalance of cell 'care' creates an environment of tissues with great strength next to tissues of profound weakness. If you look in the mirror and have rounded shoulders, or you look down to your feet and your knees are facing towards each other, you are looking at the results of an imbalance of cell loading. If every picture tells a story, so too does every human body: its very own story of how much, and how little, the cells have been affected by how they have been moved.

GRAVITY, LOADS AND THE SHAPE OF YOUR BONES

It's possibly not every day that you spend much time considering the shape of your bones, and you would be forgiven for thinking that they are a fixed, immovable feature of the body whose shape cannot be influenced. However, your bones are also constantly being affected by the loads the body experiences, both via gravity and via the soft tissues that act upon them.

Gravity

Gravity is constantly loading your body and is therefore always having an effect on your body. The best way for the body to resist this force in order to maintain form (and therefore function) is via your bones as they are the strongest, least malleable tissue of the body. The purpose of bones is to maintain the structure of your physical form and to realize the movement potential given to them by your muscles. Every bone in your body has a unique architecture depending on its location. As the saying goes, 'structure governs function' so the shape and size of each bone depends on how much load it is expected to take, and the joint with which each bone articulates dictates how much movement it has to allow.

The force of gravity occurs vertically; Newton's apple didn't fall off the tree at an angle. This exertion of force that can change the shape of the human body is best counteracted by resistance, and bones can only resist gravity in the best way if they are aligned vertically. When bones are stacked correctly, the loading they receive encourages more bone cells to be laid down, which increases their strength and density.

If, however, your bones are not stacked in alignment, gravity starts designing the shape of your body, often without you realizing it. If you are finding it difficult to imagine how an invisible force can create structural change, think about the shape of trees by the coast. The loads created by powerful ocean winds will bend the trees over so that they look like they are constantly in a wind tunnel. Gravity can do the same to your body.

So does any of this really matter? Well, yes. If, on the ground, you move yourself through the day in a posture that is not vertically aligned to gravity, you become like one of those coastal trees: a bit bent out of shape. You then take that position into the saddle and finding the position of your dreams becomes just that – a dream.

Loads

As well as gravity, your body experiences loads from other 'sources', whether it is just the load of your bodyweight or what and how you are carrying 'things'. If you carry your loads in the same way every day, you are shaping your body in a way that will affect how it sits in the saddle. How you carry the saddle, how you groom, how you tack up, how you muck out, all matters to your body. The likelihood is you will do them all the same way, loading the same structures over and over again and leaving others unused. You now know that your movement patterns shape your body and the shape your body is in will determine a number of your experiences, such as how much pain you are in, whether your lower back greets you every morning or your shoes are rubbing on that bunion or maybe you can't look over your shoulder.

So the question is, do you like or want the shape you are creating? How different would it be for your body if you changed how you loaded it? It doesn't necessarily mean that one way is better than another; the important thing is that the loads are carried *differently*.

CIRCULATION AND MOVEMENT

Most people know that the heart pumps blood around the body to service tissues, organs and systems with nutrients, and to pick up and remove the waste that they generate. However, this relatively straightforward idea is only one part (albeit significant) of your body's circulatory story.

It is estimated that an adult's circulatory system is 60,000 miles long. To service the entire area requires a complex network of

LOADS AND CELLS

Loads placed on the body via movement translate into loads on the cells themselves. This creates cellular data and this is where change in strength, density and shape occurs.

blood vessels arranged into an intricate web of delivery highways that start as large vessels as they leave the heart and become smaller and smaller towards the extremities so that every nook and cranny of the body is looked after.

The heart pumps blood around the body at rest with a heart rate that depends on your level of fitness and the 'cleanliness' of your blood vessels. It will then increase its delivery of blood flow by increasing how fast it beats as the demand becomes greater, which is what happens when the body is moving.

Homo sapiens evolved as an animal that relies on constant and varying movement for survival. Some of this movement would be slow and careful and some would be rapid and strenuous (sprints/climbing). The degree of complexity, speed and power of the movement the body was performing determined how much of the musculo-skeletal system needed to be used. When skeletal muscles are working, they lengthen and contract, sometimes slowly but consistently and at other times, such as when sprinting, much more rapidly. In times of maximum output, the muscles require a rapid delivery of nutrients coupled with a reliable waste transportation system to allow muscles to keep moving. Relying on the heart to deliver sufficient blood flow to all the working muscles under such intense circumstances would be a risky strategy. This is why the very

action of muscles changing length helps to support the delivery of blood. As they contract and lengthen, blood is pulled in and then pushed out, servicing the cells of the muscle as it works. When a muscle is repeatedly not moved, the cells start to starve from a lack of input from movement, but also from a lack of nutrient delivery in the blood. If there is no change in length of the muscle fibres, there are no mechanics to help direct blood flow towards it. If the same movement patterns are performed every day, over a period of time the way the body arranges itself will show the result of cell death in the form of muscle atrophy (wastage).

Circulation is inhibited through any static positioning of the body and through direct pressure from external forces, but also from forces experienced within the body. The route your blood vessels have to take can vary depending on the geometry of your body. For example, sitting down forces the blood vessels to curve around and zigzag over the bones of the hips, creating some narrowing and pinching of the size of the blood vessel as it presses over bone. Blood is meant to travel smoothly through your veins and arteries like melted butter along a silk road! Kinks in the road or blockages (caused by plaque, or pressure from visceral fat) can cause the blood to 'spurt'. This turbulence sends the blood crashing into the walls of the blood vessels,

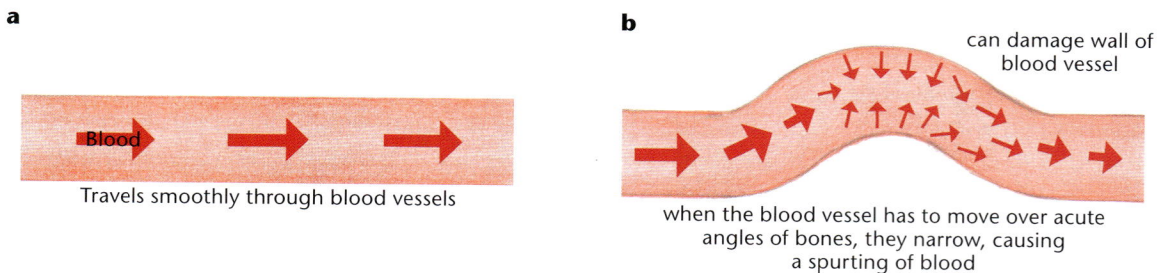

a

Blood

Travels smoothly through blood vessels

b

can damage wall of blood vessel

when the blood vessel has to move over acute angles of bones, they narrow, causing a spurting of blood

Fig. 1   Circulation and blood vessels.
a) Blood travels smoothly along a wide blood vessel that is not compromised through acute angles of bones.
b) Any narrowing of the blood vessel as it travels over bones causes blood to spurt and cause damage to the walls of the blood vessel.

which can cause damage and over time may wear the walls too thin. The body decides it needs to protect the walls so it sends cells to lay down material. This creates a thickening in the blood vessel, closing the gap for the flow of blood even further. All of a sudden the body is at risk of cardiovascular disease, even though there is nothing wrong with the heart.

YOUR HORSE'S CELLS

Your horse's body responds to movement and loads in the same way as yours does. If you ride with any area of the horse's body held in too much tension, the muscles in that area will not receive the input they need to stay healthy, and will therefore waste away.

JOINTS

Muscles might be the workers of the body, but it is the joints that turn their efforts into realized action. Muscles attach to bones via tendons, so when a muscle contracts it exerts a force/load onto the tendon, which in turn creates sufficient strength to move the bone from one position to another. Joints are formed between two (or more) bones to provide a point of mobility in the body to ensure smooth and energy-efficient travel. The architecture of each joint is determined by its location, the amount of force it is expected to receive, the direction of stressors it is likely to experience and the amount of movement that is required. The bones of a joint are held together by soft tissue structures known as ligaments. These strong, fibrous tissues act in a similar way to the stabilizers a child has on a bicycle, providing enough support to prevent chronic displacement (tipping over) and enabling the child to move forward with confidence. The

same is true for joints. If ligaments are of the optimal length, they encourage the full range of movement of the joint by providing a safe and supportive environment within which the bones are suspended. Joints will only feel safe to move if they first feel stabilized. Ligaments are not designed to deal with load in the same way that muscles are. Muscles have a much higher elasticity, which means they are able to adapt for a much longer time to load and still spring back to their normal length. Ligaments can be stretched through load, but do not have enough 'spring' to rebound back to their starting length. This means that once a ligament is lax, it will always be lax. If you have twisted your ankle once, chances are you have twisted it twice.

As with muscles, joints require movement to stay healthy. They need to do the work they were designed to do; they need to experience load, force and articulation to maintain integrity, stay lubricated and to challenge their stabilizers (ligaments) to become strong and supportive. The genius of the body is that when it is put into an optimal biomechanic position and all of these moving parts combine, the balance of work share throughout the body is just right.

Problems occur when the body's loading share is unequally distributed, and placed over joints not designed to take load. This occurs when the body is not moved from an aligned position.

THE MOVEMENT HABIT

The way you use and move your body comes down to habitually formed patterns. This is the reason people walk with a limp long after the actual symptoms of their injury have gone. The limp becomes a movement habit, which requires conscious effort to change.

Repetitive movement becomes a vicious cycle for the body. The way you stand and move will be in a posture that your body has found to be the most economical in terms of energy saving, the most comfortable and 'normal' for it. This doesn't mean it is the best position for your body to be in, but that it feels so normal that you are not drawn to adjust it.

If you have ever been repositioned on your horse, you will likely have had the experience of feeling very 'odd', off-balance, wrong. This highlights how the body and the mind trick us into believing that our habit of misalignment is correct.

SKELETAL MUSCLE MECHANICS

'A tight muscle will pull a joint into a dysfunctional position, and a weak muscle will allow this to happen.'

To understand the implications of poor movement, it is necessary to have an understanding of what happens at a cellular level within your muscles. Each muscle is an all-encompassing unit containing smaller and smaller segments that enable the muscle to do its job.

Muscles are an exceptional piece of kit. They adapt to the positions they find themselves in, they work hard, and they help each other out. If they are used they grow, and if they are neglected they shrink. Life becomes really difficult when the adaptations required are too severe, or the workload is too heavy, as although muscles are magnificent at adapting, their ability to compromise is not endless.

The whole premise of skeletal muscle mechanics is that they maintain the right length to be able to move a bone. Optimal length describes the ideal resting length from which it can contract or lengthen. Skeletal muscles (those involved in moving

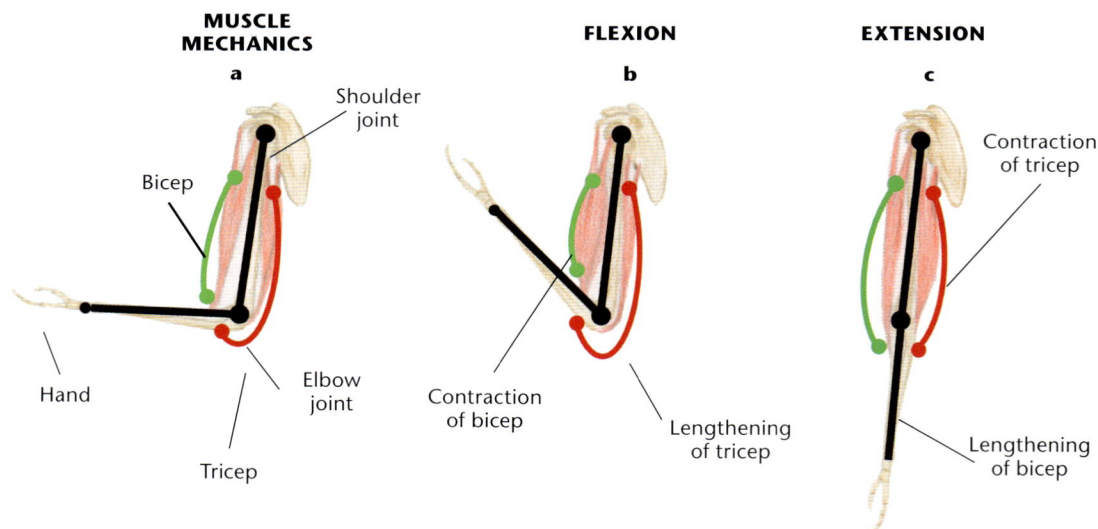

Fig. 2   Muscle mechanics.
a) *The elbow joint in a neutral position showing the biceps at the front of the joint and the triceps at the back.*
b) *Flexion of the elbow joint showing contraction of the biceps and reciprocal lengthening of the triceps.*
c) *Extension of the elbow joint showing contraction of the tricep muscle group and reciprocal lengthening of the biceps.*

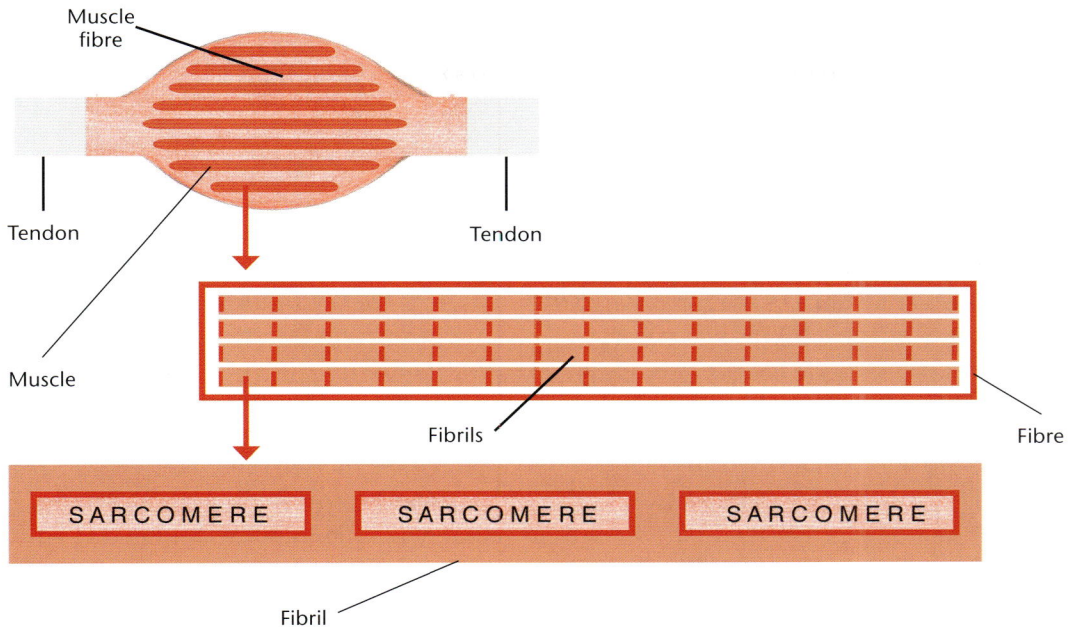

Fig. 3   Muscle anatomy. A look inside the belly of a muscle to show the rows of fibres, the fibrils within the fibre and the sections of sarcomeres.

your bones) work as teams. There are muscles on either side of your joints, and when one shortens to move the bone, the muscle on the other side of the joint has to lengthen. This can be shown by the biceps (front of your upper arm from elbow to shoulder) and the triceps (back of your upper arm, elbow to shoulder).

MUSCLE ANATOMY

To really grasp the concept of the importance of movement, it is necessary to know how a muscle responds to movement, and in order to do that you need to get to the deepest, smallest segment that controls how muscles work on a cellular level.

The muscle puzzle is a layering system of ever-decreasing structures. The contour or shape you might see on a well-defined body

is the end result of all these layers. If you were to take a peek inside, the first thing you would see would be bundles of fibres. These are individual rope-like structures that sit in uniform rows, one on top of the other. These are the largest segment of skeletal muscle. Within each fibre are smaller ropes known as fibrils. And if you look inside a fibril, you will see segments known as sarcomeres. But the story doesn't end there, as to get to the heart of the muscle narrative you have to go one level deeper and look inside a sarcomere.

THE MAGIC WITHIN A SARCOMERE

Within each sarcomere (which are separate compartments along the length of the fibril, which are the length of the fibres, which give the muscle its shape and length) is the hub of intelligence, control and movement potential. Within each sarcomere are sections of proteins – actin and myosin – which enable the muscle to move.

Actin

The outer protein sections of the sarcomere are known as actin. Imagine this as two halves of a rectangle which are able to slide over each other.

Myosin

The proteins on the inside are known as myosin. The myosin proteins are attached to the actin by a spring-like structure called titin (*see* Fig. 4).

When the brain sends an instruction for the muscle to contract, the myosin are activated (via units of energy) to bring both sides of the actin closer together. Each myosin should have contact with the actin for maximum force generation. As the actin moves closer together, the spring on the end of the 'box' is stretched, and then recoils to allow the sarcomere to return to resting length; in other words, to move the box back to where it started. For the best movement potential, as many myosin as possible need to have contact with the actin.

When a muscle is held in a habitually shortened position through postural habits, the actin overlap each other when they are meant to be in their 'resting' position. This means that when the muscle is required to contract to create movement, there is no 'movement potential'; quite simply, there is no space to move into.

Muscles are great adaptors, so where one might be sitting in a shortened state, there will

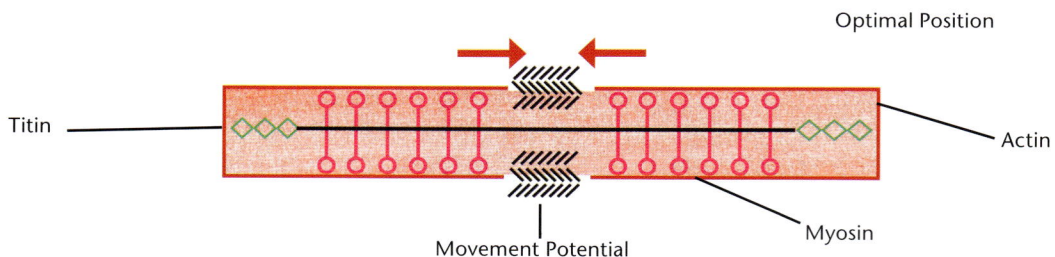

Fig. 4 *The components of a sarcomere, including the proteins actin and myosin sitting in a normal resting length.*

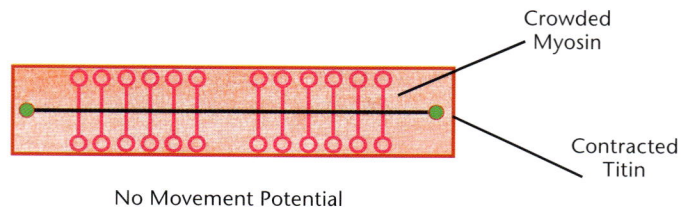

Fig. 5 *Shortened sarcomere. The appearance of a sarcomere that has no movement potential; notice the actin have slid completely over each other*

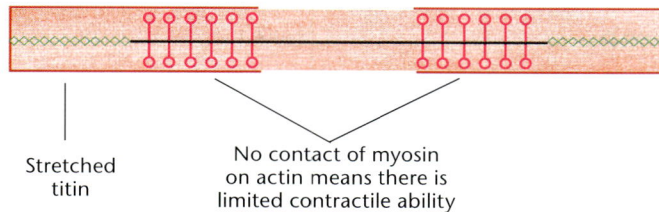

Stretched titin

No contact of myosin on actin means there is limited contractile ability

Fig. 6 The appearance of a sarcomere that has been stretched. Notice that the myosin have lost contact with the actin and will therefore be unable to bring the actin closer together.

be another in a state of chronic lengthening. Fig. 6 shows a sarcomere that is sitting in a habitually lengthened position.

Here you can see that only a few of the myosin have any contact with the actin as it has been stretched too far. This means that the force of the contraction will be very weak. In chronic situations the muscle fibres have been stretched so far that none of the myosin are touching the actin, which means that there is no force production at all.

Research in human muscle science has found that muscles which sit in a constant position, whether that be short or stretched, will change the number of sarcomeres within the fibril to ensure the body is able to be moved. To be static would be detrimental for survival so there needs to be a way for the body to ensure its muscles can continue to generate force from whatever position they find themselves in. This means that the number of sarcomeres within a fibril is changeable at a cellular level.

If a shortened muscle has sarcomeres that are all sitting in an overlapped position and have nowhere to move, the muscle will remove one or more sarcomeres to give the remaining ones space to move. So now a shortened muscle has been shortened on a biological level. Likewise, a muscle that is stretched and weakened will gain one or more blocks of sarcomeres to fill in the space and move the actin back over the myosin. This leaves a stretched muscle even longer. The situation is

no longer a temporary, adaptable arrangement and the body is left in a state of more imbalance within the tissues, and a dangerous cycle of poor movement is enhanced.

These patterns occur when the body is moved out of alignment as a recurring theme all day, every day. Footwear and time spent in static positions are all responsible for demanding this level of adaptability within the tissues of the body. It is the reason why women who wear high heels for a number of years end up not able to walk with their heels on the ground.

So why does knowing this help you?

The impact of how you are moving through the day is probably greater than you have ever considered. By having an appreciation of the position you hold your body in all of the time, you will start to paint a picture of the shape of the body you are bringing to the saddle, and why some positional faults might be creeping in.

A SENSITIVE SUBJECT – SENSORY INPUT

'The rabbit hole is not the problem. The problem is the body not being able to cope with the rabbit hole.'

Movement not only changes the length, shape and function of your soft tissues and joints, but also serves the body on a whole other level, which is neural and sensory. Movement in different planes, in a variety of postures, over different terrains, carrying, jumping, climbing, swinging and balancing all provide the body with a matrix of sensory input. This develops neural pathways that increase the body's ability to understand where it is in time and space, which is known as proprioception and is necessary for balanced, economic and safe movement. It is the neural pathways that save you from twisting your ankle in a divot, or allow you to save yourself when you trip over. Movement provides the body with intelligence on how to navigate the environment. This is a 'learn on the job' scenario; you can't read your way to great proprioception. You have to fall in the rabbit hole, trip over the bamboo cane and slip on the banana skin to build the infrastructure between brain and body so that when you find those obstacles again, your body's reaction keeps you out of the doctor's surgery. Riding is a highly proprioceptive sport; it relies heavily on the body's ability to synthesize a huge amount of sensory and neural input. The difference between a riding and a non-riding life is that the pelvis becomes the new base of support in the saddle, as opposed to the feet. Building neural pathways on the ground relies on the reflex system of the core (*see* Chapter 2) to be able to synthesize the information the body receives when it is in the saddle. This only happens if the body is moved in different ways during the day, so building these proprioceptive pathways 'off-horse' is critical to improving matters in the saddle.

Every joint is responsible for its own integrity. This means that the ligaments and neural receptors within the joint capsule are responsible for constant dialogue through the nervous system, to tell the brain which position they are in and therefore what

muscular support they need. When these channels of neuro signals are awake and fit, they are as sensitive as a hormonal teenager, reacting instantly to the slightest change in their environment. It is this sensitivity that corrects your foot on uneven ground, stabilizes your knees, hips and spine, changes the speed of joint articulation dependent upon terrain or activity and does a big job in keeping you upright when you take any step at all. The importance of conditioning this intrinsic support system is likened to having a solid foundation for your house. We are probably all familiar with the analogy yet most of us have not been taught how to strengthen from the inside out.

The body you build in terms of shape, function, adaptability, pain levels and injury potential is all down to the repetitive movements you do and the position you hold it in. This determines which muscles you use, setting in motion the health (length) of these muscles and therefore the health of the joint that they manage. In real terms, this creates the difference between weight-lifters, ballerinas, gymnasts, sprinters, marathon runners and horse-riders. The shape and subsequent function of their bodies are entirely different because of how they have repeatedly been used.

When you see a weight-lifter, the first word into your mind to describe them will likely be something to do with strength, rather than flexible or supple. By contrast, when you see a gymnast, you are more likely to describe them as being super-flexible, strong, supple and controlled. If we watch a ballerina, we marvel at the control and grace of their movement. When you see a good rider, you see poise and balance. Like a gymnast or a ballerina, it is the intrinsic strength – in other words, the strength of their foundation – that enables the athlete to look controlled in their movements and allows the rider to sit in synchronicity with the horse's movement.

A weight-lifter will focus their training on brawn – pure strength and explosive power. The muscles bind the joints to limit movement and, although their strength is clear to see, they would find it very difficult to sit in synchronicity with a horse. Why? Their joints are being held in place by extreme muscle mass, which means they have a very small chance of oscillation. Tension at both sides of a joint removes its freedom to move, and it can no longer be suspended in the sling of ligaments or fascia as it was designed to be.

Riding requires the entire body to be strong, in all planes of movement, and to be truly strong the joints first have to feel safe to move, and then actually be able to move. An unstable joint whose ligaments have not been strengthened through correct movement, or a joint that is not aligned correctly, will require more muscular support for it to feel stable. This means the muscles affecting the bones of the joint are required to support it through being contracted and in a static state. This creates tension as it disables the joint *and* the muscle from moving freely. A joint that is unable to 'oscillate' in response to movement or sensory input is at a huge disadvantage for riding. Research has shown that more 'elite' riders are able to absorb the horse's movements through their joints oscillating in harmony throughout their body, from ankles to wrists to elbows. It is very difficult to free up a joint in the saddle to absorb and cope with the magnitude of sensory input if it has been held in place by a tense muscle on the ground. Many riding positional faults can be attributed to joints that are unable to move and respond to proprioceptive signals.

2 How Your Body was Built to Move: Understanding the System

Around 200,000 years ago the first modern humans walked in a body mechanically identical to the one you inhabit today. This is not an insignificant fact! The way your body is designed to be moved has not changed for a *very* long time. Evolution led the human species to be an animal capable of innovation and creation, to have a level of logical, problem-solving intelligence, rationality and the desire for growth. This level of thinking was far beyond that of any other species on the planet, but where intelligence excelled, aspects of the physical body left humans vulnerable. The need to manufacture heat, protect a digestive tract through cooking meat and sourcing a varied diet, through to the need to build protective shelters dictated a lifestyle that revolved around movement. Movement to forage and hunt for food, movement to source water, movement to make fire, to cook, to migrate, to push, to carry, to balance, to climb, to walk, to run. For about eight hours a day the body had to withstand movement in various positions with joints and soft tissues tackling different loads. Resting time was also important as it gave the body time to heal and rejuvenate, but sleeping as your distant ancestors would have done, without a soft, comfortable, body-contouring mattress to hug and cushion the body, meant that it received yet even more loads for even more time. This continual cycle of squashing, bending and changing the shape of cells was how the body evolved to thrive from movement, and it was this dependence upon movement that dictated the mechanical make-up of the body. It is not by chance that the hips are the largest joint of the body or that the spine is arranged into curves, for example. Your body is a container that has been moulded over millennia to be strong, mobile and as resistant to injury as possible. It was born from the powerful need for survival within a lifestyle of self-sufficiency, which created a machine of engineering brilliance.

Movement for the body worked so well because daily activities created a tiered, or hierarchical, system. The basic positions used for meal preparation and toileting, and the regular periods of walking, bending, reaching and carrying, all prepared the musculo-skeletal system in the detail of movement; the small, precise, aligned protocols that were performed each day for a lot of the day set the foundation for withstanding the rigours of big, bold, explosive moves that were also a necessary part of life. The 'good old days' were really days based around a 'movement pick and mix', creating an operating manual for the body that kept it strong, mobile and pain-free. The problem is, you or your parents or your grandparents have never been shown this operating manual and it isn't hiding in the kitchen drawer alongside the instructions for the microwave. The rapid change in how humans lived changed the way the body was used and the laws of human biomechanics were lost at the bottom of the pile of machinery and technology. Modern movement has not considered the fundamental make-up of how the body was designed or for what environment it was intended to thrive in. Great, sustainable movement is like an ancient language that has been forgotten and as a result modern societies are suffering from diseases of poor movement more than ever before. With the escalation of 'convenience' and the rise of increasingly sophisticated technology, there doesn't appear to be an environment waiting around the corner to help 'fix' the global movement deficit. The answer is to provide yourself with an understanding of the operating manual of the body. Knowing how it is designed and how the system is meant to be used will empower you to make small, consistent changes that have the potential to change your life. Moving without pain, avoiding surgery, maintaining your activity levels and improving your position and effectiveness in the saddle are all possible with some knowledge and tools. This chapter will take you through the body in the way that it was designed to function. You will see that the body is connected, from the jaw to the hips and the hips to the feet, so that even though segments will be explained individually, it should not be forgotten that they all have a connection to one another.

OPERATING MANUAL: THE HUMAN BODY

The importance of vertical alignment

The human body evolved with movement at the core of survival, so it stands to reason that the body was designed to be moved within certain parameters that served its engineering design and that kept it moving happily. A key part of making sure the body remained a proficient machine for survival was how it coped with hours of weight-bearing on the legs and feet, how well oxygen could get into the lungs, how strong the spine was and how muscles maintained their optimal length to enable movement. All of these factors relied on one biomechanical factor, and that is how the body was *aligned*.

Moving the body from a place of alignment is the cornerstone of human biomechanics. Alignment means that each part of the body is in the correct place, relative to every other part. The human body is a collection of independent parts that are designed to come together and work cohesively as a whole unit, therefore by moving each part in alignment with every other, it is possible to build a sustainable and pain-free movement machine.

Vertical alignment

As described in Chapter 1, the body is constantly responding to the pull of gravity, and the most efficient place to do this from is in a position of vertical alignment. Being vertically aligned means that the bones are perpendicular to the gravitational force, giving them the best chance of resisting gravity and building density and strength. Aligning the body vertically also ensures that the correct structures are loaded with weight, the right amount of movement at joints is possible and muscular force is at its best. The pelvis is a major influencer of movement and mechanics as it is the body's centre of mass, the 'house' for the hip joint and the connector of the upper body with the lower. The hip joints are the largest in the body and as such are designed to take the most load. Their architecture also allows them a large amount of movement. Where they sit, in relation to the shoulders above and the heels below, will dictate how much load they carry and how much of this movement they will be able to realize. Vertical alignment requires that the shoulders, hips and heels are stacked on top of one another – a fortuitous alliance with the position required in the saddle – and it determines everything from how the body can move across the ground, to how healthy the joints are, to how strong the muscles are, to how stable the spine is, to how the arms can move and how the body can breathe.

The human body is designed for forward movement across the ground – a staple feature for the hunter-gatherer lifestyle of old. For this reason the muscles at the back of the body are designed to be strong – to push, pull and carry with a strong, well supported spine and the powerful forward-driving muscles of the glutes and the hamstrings. The spine is not a self-supporting structure, so it relies upon muscular strength to maintain its shape, its ability to move and its neurological integrity.

These features all arose from a body in the correct vertical alignment. Being in the right position meant that every move it was required to do actually helped the body become stronger and more mobile. This means that it is also the best place to be in to prepare your body for riding.

The following pages will explore the different components of the body, how they are designed anatomically and how they were designed to be used. By understanding the system that is your body, you will be able to interact with it in a way that leads you to make small but positive changes in how you move, which will lead to positive changes in the saddle.

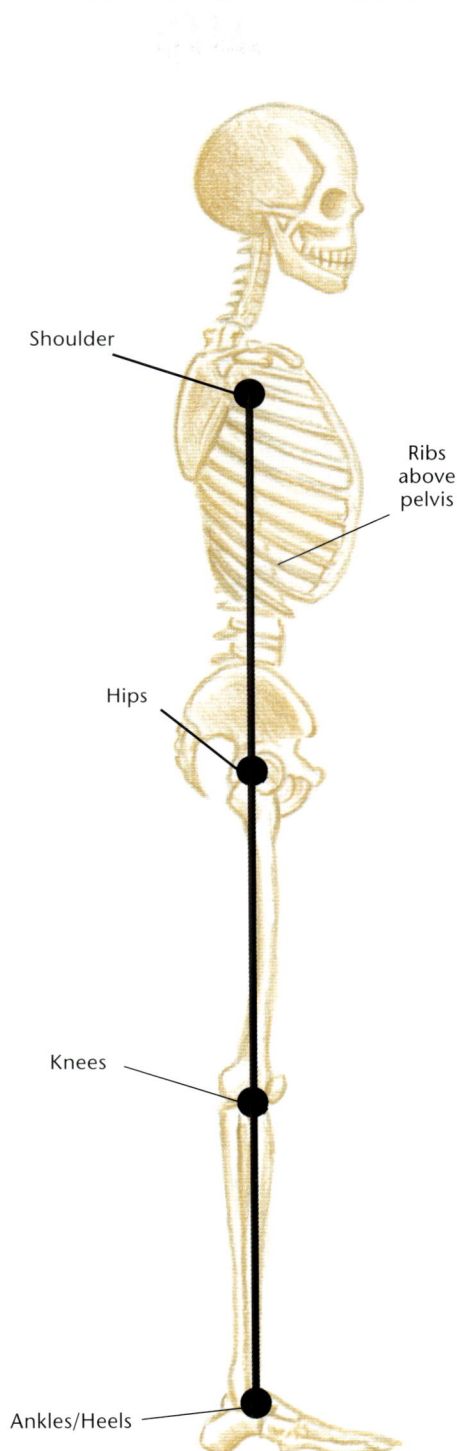

Fig. 7   Vertical alignment with shoulders, ribs, hips and heels in line.

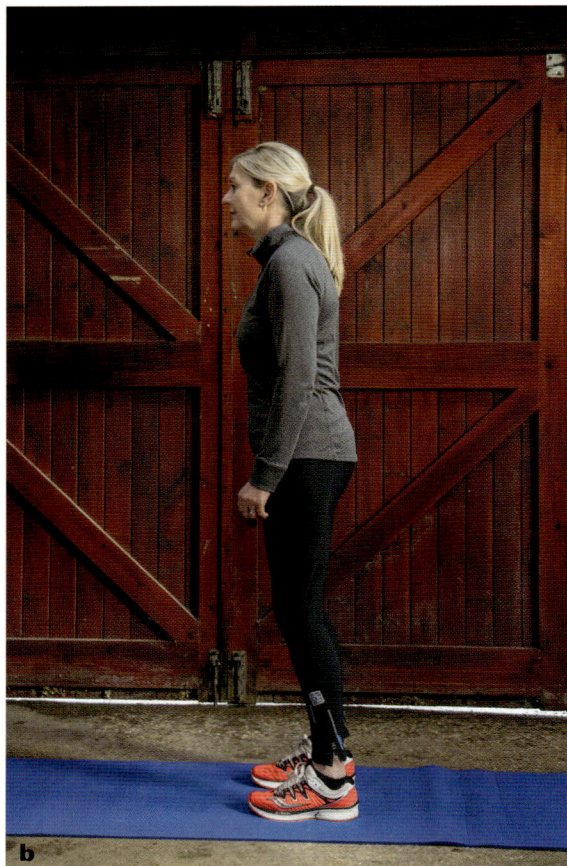

a) Standing in vertical alignment; the pelvis and hips are over the heels, the ribs are in line with the front of the pelvis, the shoulders are in line with the ribs and the chin is pulled close to the neck. b) Notice the contrast of what has become a 'normal' posture.

Ground reaction force and kinetic chains

To understand the importance of alignment, it is helpful to have an understanding of what the body has to do every time your foot hits the ground. Ground Reaction Force (GRF) is the ground's response to an applied load. So when you place your foot down and apply force through your leg into the ground, the ground will apply a force back to you in equal measure. How your body receives this force depends upon its alignment. To deal with gravity in the best way, your bones need to be in vertical

alignment, so it makes sense to understand that receiving a load in the opposite direction would benefit from an aligned position too. Stacking the body vertically ensures that the load you give to the ground, and the one you receive back, is delivered in a way that you can carry without causing damage. It doesn't have to be about the magnitude of a load, just as it doesn't have to be about weight. What is important is *how* you are carrying the weight across the ground and the impact it is going to have on your body.

In relation to ground reaction force there is a process known as 'kinetic chains'. This refers to

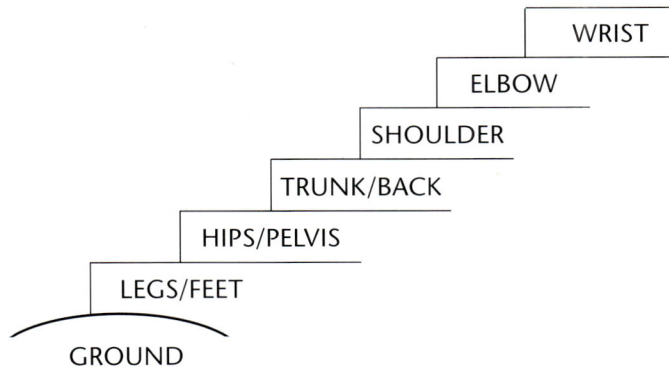

Fig. 8 *Kinetic chains. The chain of effect when one area of the body is not working as well as it should.*

the fact that if one element of your body isn't working, it increases the chance of a problem elsewhere, further up the chain. In terms of GRF, if the legs are unable to cope, it goes to the hips, then the trunk and the back and on up the body.

foundation for the spine to extend from and the vehicle for linking the upper body with the legs. Biomechanically, every movement you make has to pass through the pelvis; from walking to sitting, standing to running, jumping to climbing, the pelvis

THE COMPONENTS THAT MAKE THE WHOLE

The pelvis

In a discussion about how the human body was designed to function, the pelvis may seem like an odd place to begin. On the surface of things, the head or the feet may appear a more logical starting point, but the pelvis is the mothership of the body, both biomechanically and physiologically, and therefore it goes at the top of the list.

The pelvis (from the Latin word meaning 'basin') is a three-dimensional bowl that is the body's centre of mass. It is the

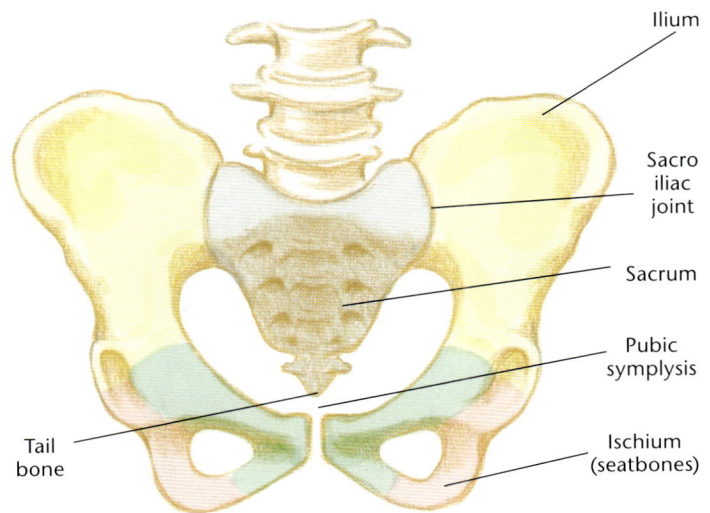

Fig. 9 *The skeletal structure of the pelvis (front view), showing the bones and joints that make up the pelvic girdle.*

receives load and information from every movement. Riding uses the pelvis as the base of support for the body, and all the information the body requires to stay in the saddle has to come through the pelvis. The skeletal framework creates the shape of the bowl, and to ensure it can accommodate the mechanic of the entire body, this principal segment relies on a matrix of soft tissues including ligaments, muscles and fascia to keep it in a balanced, level position.

The pelvic girdle: designed to conquer

Structurally, the pelvic girdle is created by three pairs of bones (one on each side) and two single bones. The largest pair of bones are the ilia (sing. ilium), which are fan-shaped and are the bones you feel when you put your hands on your hips. These create around 40 per cent of the socket for the hip joint and provide a large surface area for muscle attachments.

The next in size are the ischium, commonly known as the seat bones and an area that is well known to riders. These sit beneath the ilium and make up another 40 per cent of the hip socket.

The final pair of pelvic bones lie at the front and bottom of the pelvic bowl. These are the pubic bones, which are connected by a broad, flat piece of fibrocartilage known as the pubic symphysis. The pubic bones make up the remaining 20 per cent of the hip socket.

At the back of the pelvis is the sacrum. This is a triangular-shaped piece of bone that is made from five bones fused together. This bone 'floats' in-between the two ilia, connected to them by ligaments. It is this connection between sacrum and ilia that creates the sacroiliac joint. This joint is designed to allow a small amount of movement between the sacrum and the large pelvic bones, but its connection to the pelvis is only as strong as the ligaments that attach it. These joints are at the mercy of loading patterns of the feet and legs, the positioning of the pelvis, and how the pelvis interacts with the lumbar spine. The final piece of the pelvis is the coccyx, also known as the tailbone. This is the continuation and end point of the spine and provides an important attachment point for the muscles of the pelvic floor.

In terms of muscular support, thirty-five muscles attach on or around the pelvis, all of which are designed to apply equal loads in different directions to keep the pelvis in an aligned and what is termed today as

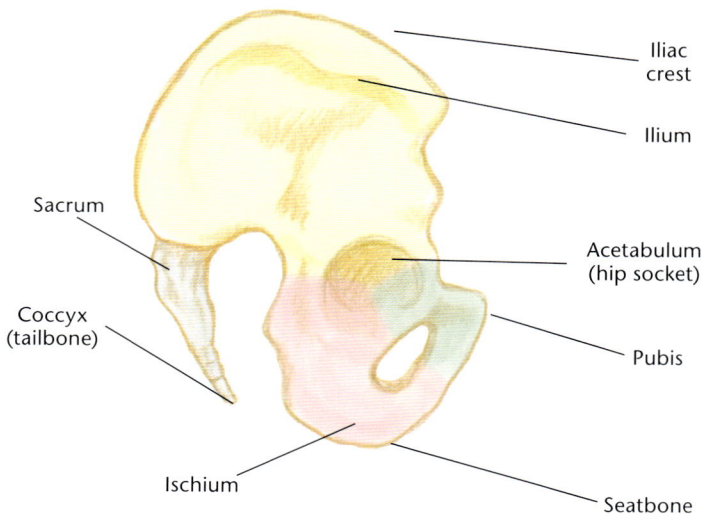

Fig. 10   Side view of the bones of the pelvis, showing how the acetabulum is created.

FIBROCARTILAGE

Fibrocartilage is a dense matrix of collagen fibres designed to absorb shock in areas where excessive pressures are generated. It is found in the pubic symphysis and the intervertebral discs.

a 'neutral' position, which means to keep the bowl level. These muscles behave like guy ropes on a tent whose job is to keep the tent upright whatever forces might apply load to it (i.e. wind). This is only possible if there is equal tension through each rope. If one slackens off, the tent is vulnerable to being shifted out of position, and the same is true for the pelvis. If one muscle is tighter than the other, the bowl is vulnerable to being tipped out of balance.

As the centre of mass for the body, and the channel through which all movement passes, the pelvic region evolved to thrive from being in different positions for a number of hours during the day. These various postures kept the soft tissues constantly adapting and responding to different loads, which kept them healthy enough to keep the position of the pelvis balanced, allowed movement of the hip joint, stabilized movement at the sacroiliac joint and balanced how the pelvis moved in relation to the thighs and lower back. This fairly consistent loading of the body was done via the feet (standing, squatting, walking), which also meant that the muscles at the bottom of the pelvis (pelvic floor) received loads through downward pressure within the pelvic cavity, which helped to keep them toned and

healthy. Our ancestors would have walked for ten to twelve miles a day in bare feet, often carrying children, water, wood or food. Walking was as fundamental to life as breathing and it is still as much a part of your DNA as the colour of your eyes. The pelvis would have been loaded with the weight of the upper body over the large and load-bearing hip joints, the hips would have had a full range of movement from walking, squatting and climbing, and the feet would have interacted with the ground directly without the barrier of shoes. This meant the feet were strong, wide, dextrous and supple, with a very

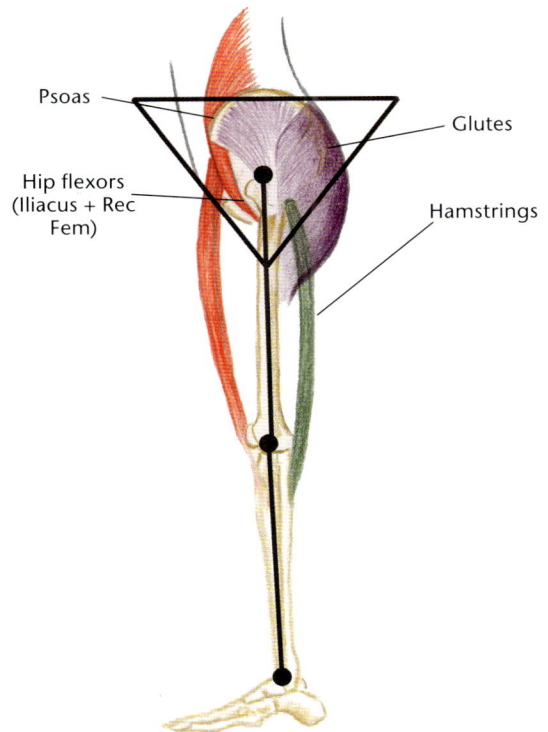

Fig. 11 Key muscles of the pelvis. These muscles are the most significant to the function of the pelvis, and for you as a rider: the glutes, hamstrings, psoas and hip flexors.

efficient communication system to the brain regarding where they were in time and space. All of these lifestyle practices kept the soft tissues that control the position of the pelvis healthy by placing them under an optimal amount of load.

THE IMPORTANCE OF NEUTRAL

As the pelvis is such an influential segment of the body, its position in relation to the ground and to the legs and spine is critical to the overall success of how the whole body functions. Sitting in alignment means that the pelvis is also in a 'neutral' position.

Considering the pelvis as a bowl, the neutral position is when this bowl is level horizontally and vertically. If you can imagine it full of water, a neutral pelvis would hold all the water inside without tipping any out at the front, back or sides. This position has three points of reference (when considering neutral relative to the ground):

- The two ilia (wing bones of the pelvis; where you would place your hands on your hips) should align vertically with

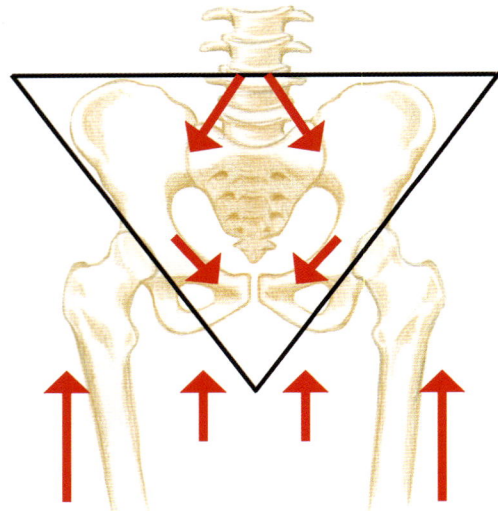

Fig. 12   The direction of all the loads the pelvis has to facilitate, including external loads from the limbs and internal loads through downward pressure of the pelvic and abdominal cavities.

- the pubic symphysis, at the front and bottom of the pelvis, which should align horizontally with
- the coccyx (tailbone) at the back of the pelvis.

PROPRIOCEPTION

Proprioception refers to the ability of one part of your body to know where it is in time and space, relative to the other parts of your body. When a joint or muscle moves out of position, the receivers of this information (proprioceptors) relay it to the brain so that it can form an 'image' of what is happening internally within the tissues and decide the best course of action. The aim is always to respond in a way that is the least damaging to the tissues, so having a clear image of what is happening is really important. Communication – and therefore image creation – is improved when muscles are of a healthy tone and the joints they are working with are not stiff. Tight muscles and stiff joints do not allow the proprioceptors to gather enough information, so the image can be grainy and incomplete. The response from the brain is always going to be a bit hit and miss in this case, as it is not able to be clear about the exact positioning of the tissues.

The neutral pelvis and the hip joint

The hip joint is made from the head of the femur (thigh bone) and the acetabulum (the socket), which as you have seen is made from the meeting of the ilium, the ischium and the pubic bone.

When truly in neutral, the femur will drop vertically from the hip socket, keeping the head of the femur in the centre. In this position, the hip is capable of the full range of movement as there is space in front of it and behind it within the joint capsule. It can behave like a pendulum, travelling happily both backwards and forwards, and this is the position it needs to be in for a correct, effective leg position in the saddle. If the pelvis is moved out of neutral and tips either forwards or backwards, the hip joint and therefore the thigh can get locked into one position, which limits the potential movement the joint can achieve. This immediately changes the mechanic of every position and movement that is performed. The fallout of a lack of mobility in the hip is that the lower back will compensate, causing all sorts of problems (*see* Chapter 3).

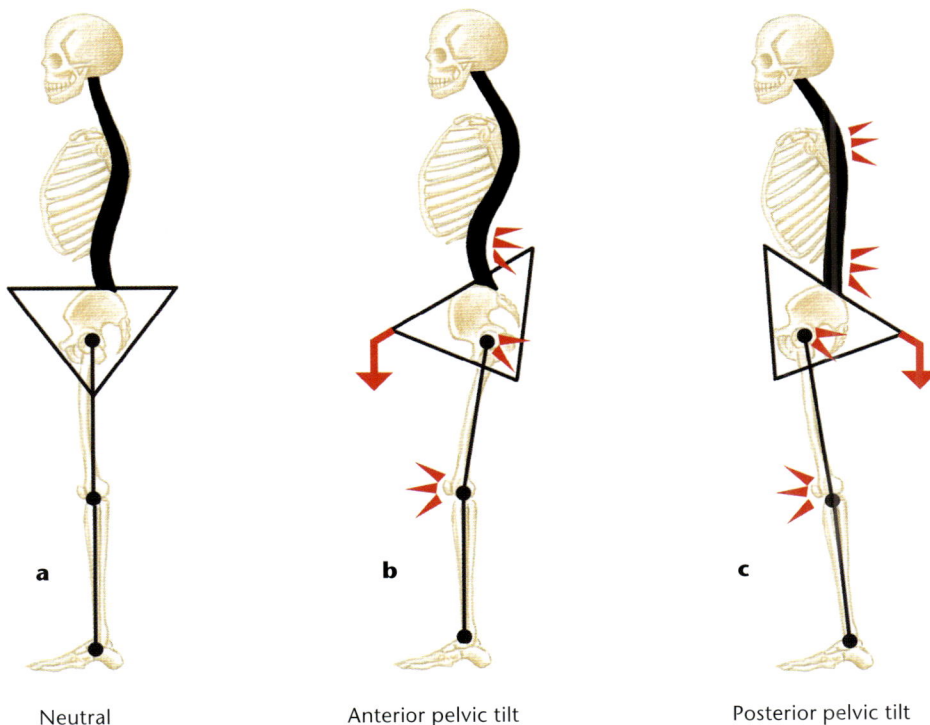

a	b	c
Neutral	Anterior pelvic tilt	Posterior pelvic tilt

Fig. 13   The positions of the pelvis.
a) The pelvis in an ideal, neutral position where the joints have maximum movement potential and receive the appropriate amount of load. The spine can maintain its natural curves.
b) Anterior pelvic tilt, where the pelvis has dropped down at the front and increased the lumbar curvature of the spine. This position loads the knees too much and restricts hip mobility.
c) Posterior pelvic tilt, where the pelvis has dropped down at the back and is tucked underneath the body. This removes the lumbar curve and places it into flexion, damaging the vertebrae.

The hip joint: anatomy and function

The design of the hip joint is such that it allows for a large amount of movement of the legs. They can move in front of the body, behind the body, across the body and away from the body, and within the socket the head of the femur can rotate internally (to face inwards) and externally (to face outwards), which is a necessity for sitting in the saddle. As well as this array of movement, the architecture of the head of the femur is large enough that it can take the most amount of load of any joint in the body.

As well as their ability to move independently, the hips also allow the pelvis to rotate over them whilst the hips themselves stay vertical. This movement provides the hips with the role of fulcrum for the body so that any forward bending of the upper body should occur from a hinging of the hips, rather than through flexion of the lower back. This mechanic is engineered so that the vulnerable joints of the lower back do not repeatedly impinge on the intervertebral discs and cause damage every time the hands need to get to the floor. Because of this movement potential and mass, the joint is supported by a web of soft tissues that are expected to stabilize and move the joint depending on the activity it is required to do.

Hip flexors

These muscles at the front of the leg attach the thigh to the pelvis. The main two hip flexors are the iliacus and the rectus femoris, which is part of the quadricep group that runs from your hip to your knee at the front of your leg. The job of these muscles is to close the angle of the hip joint (flexion) by bringing the leg in front of the body and your knee to your nose. They work reciprocally with the glutes at the back of the hip; thus, when the glutes fire,

these muscles are designed to have enough resting length to allow the hip to move into extension. When these muscles hold excessive tension, they pull the front of the pelvis down towards the thigh bones.

Psoas

The psoas ('so-as') is a mighty muscle (you have two, one either side of the spine) as it has the most bony attachments of any muscle in the body, coming in at twenty-two to twenty-four. Most of these attachments are to vertebrae, with the lowest two attaching to the thigh. Quite often the psoas gets lumbered in as a hip flexor, but in reality it actually moves the spine into flexion more than it moves the hip. It serves as a rib, spine and pelvic stabilizer and brings the lower body towards the ground. When this muscle holds excessive tension, it will bring the lumbar spine into flexion and tuck the pelvis underneath the body.

Glutes

The gluteal group comprises three muscles – the glute maximus, medius and minimus – which all affect the hip either in extension or external rotation and are, as such, essential muscles for how the body moves across the ground but also how the leg is able to be positioned in the saddle.

On the ground, these muscles are responsible for bringing the hip into extension and pushing the body forwards. They are also responsible for holding the weight of the body as it lowers into a squat or sits down, and for pushing the body back to an upright position. People who struggle to stand up without pushing off the chair with their arms are lacking in glute strength, as are those who 'fall' the last few inches as they go to sit down.

The health of the glutes is critical to the health of the hips, and full hip mobility is essential if you are going to sit in the saddle in balance and comfort, and not create damage to your hips that will affect you when you are not riding. If the glutes are already under tension because of poor hip position, asking them to rotate and extend in the saddle is going to put them under too much stress.

Healthy, strong glutes enable the rider to sit in balance, control the movement of the rising trot and help to provide strength to deliver aids through the seat to the horse. These muscles are an important member of your movement story.

RANGE OF MOVEMENT

Range of Movement (ROM) indicates how much movement a joint has relative to how much it is designed to have. It is often used as a comparative tool to assess left and right sides as part of investigative analysis of dysfunction.

Hip extension

Movement across the ground with efficiency of energy, maximum forward potential and balance relies on the ability of the leg to come behind the body and push the body forward with sufficient force. This movement involves hip extension, which recruits the glute muscles at the back and the sides of the hip, providing movement and then stability under load from the forward push. The amount of hip extension available determines how much muscle recruitment is necessary, which therefore determines how well the body is pushed across the ground.

Full hip extension is only possible when the pelvis is in neutral and the body is vertically aligned. The recruitment of the muscles of the hip is an essential part of how your body is designed to move. As the glutes switch on to move the hip behind the body, they also act as stabilizers for the sacroiliac joint. Good hip extension is a feature of a body operating from a great biomechanic, and was a key contributor to how our ancestors moved for so much of the day without succumbing to injury.

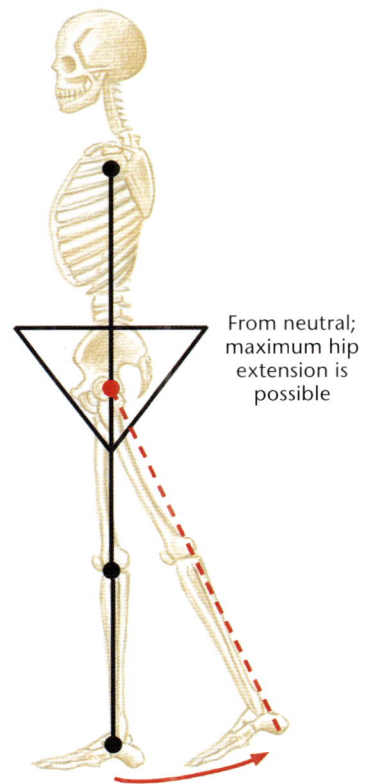

From neutral; maximum hip extension is possible

Fig. 14   *When the hip is hanging from a neutral pelvis and in the centre of the socket, it has the ability to move into extension (behind the body), which helps to strengthen and stabilize the pelvis and lower back.*

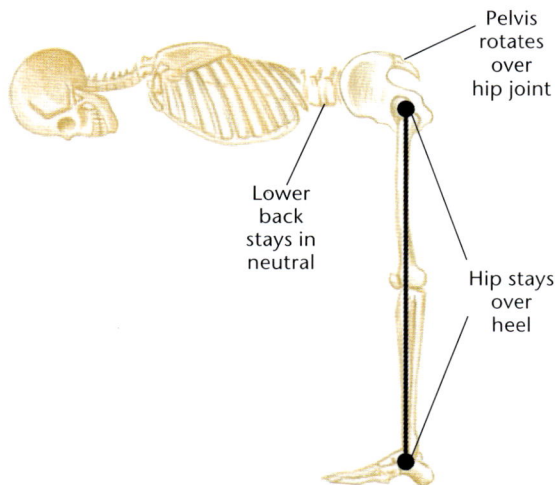

Fig. 15   The hips are designed to be the main fulcrum of the body. This shows how the pelvis should hinge over the top of the hip to create forward bend.

Independent hip movement

From a neutral pelvis the thighs are able to 'hang' vertically, with space within the hip joint for freedom of movement. In this position, the pelvis is able to remain in neutral regardless of where the leg is positioned. To put it another way, the hips can move *independently* from the pelvis and the pelvis can move independently from the hips. For a rider this independent hip movement is essential. From rising trot to jumping position to a balanced dressage seat, the hips must be able to move without influencing the neutral positioning of the pelvis. This is explored in more detail in Chapter 4.

Neutral pelvis and the muscles of the pelvic floor

The muscles of the pelvic floor attach from the coccyx at the back of the pelvis to the pubic symphysis at the front. They are the base of the core and are responsible for holding your organs within your body and for releasing and contracting your bathroom muscles as required. The tone of these muscles – their health, strength and mobility – is dependent upon the positioning of their two points of attachment at the front and back of the pelvis. Only when the pelvis is in neutral and these two points align can the pelvic floor muscles work optimally with the right length to contract and relax. The muscle fibres of the pelvic floor are the same as other skeletal muscles like the biceps in your arm, which means they strengthen by changing length in response to load. Load to the pelvic floor muscles is applied via downward pressures experienced when the body is loading the feet, as well as mechanical loads via different positions of the pelvis. Early humans maintained the strength and integrity of these muscles via their movement lifestyle. A key movement that was essential for pelvic health was the amount of time spent in a deep squat. This position not only helped to keep the hips healthy, but it also maintained flexibility in the ankles and a healthy length of muscle in the calf and decompressed the connection of the pelvis to the lumbar spine. Weakness through the pelvic floor muscles may result in a host of problems (*see* Chapter 3) and can affect the health of your lower back, your hips and your knees. In fact, if you have knee pain, the chances are you have some level of pelvic floor dysfunction too. For riders the pelvic floor muscles are vulnerable to becoming weak if a lot of time is spent in the saddle as this direct pressure from the saddle in the pelvic floor region can cause the muscles to slacken and switch off. This means that riding will not improve the tone of these muscles, so they must be strengthened off horse by the movements you do during the day.

PELVIC FLOOR EXERCISES (KEGELS)

Squeezing the muscles of the pelvic floor, or lifting them up, or holding them in any kind of contraction does not strengthen them. This contraction 'casts' them into a state of tension, which is not a strengthening posture; muscles require movement to become strong.

SQUATTING

A true squat, of the type that would have been used in real life (as opposed to the kind seen in the gym) is as fundamental to the human body as walking. This movement consists of dropping the buttocks down to the heels, with the feet flat on the floor. It is the best position for toileting and childbirth and would have been the position people maintained whilst prepping meals, making tools and eating. This frequent positioning of opening the hip joints, taking them into full flexion whilst keeping the pelvis and lower back aligned, created an environment for the pelvis and all the organs contained within the pelvis cavity to function with sufficient space but also with appropriate levels of pressure, particularly on the muscles of the pelvic floor. It was an everyday movement that sustained pelvic, hip, ankle and lower back health, but even though it is a position we were born to be able to do (take a look at any child playing), it has been lost from most adult lives in much of the developed world. As a result there are a plethora of problems with pelvic floor issues and bowel movements, as well as the mechanical nature of how the hips and pelvis should be able to move.

As an adult, the thought of getting into this type of squat might send panic waves through your body and you may well be right to think that you couldn't get into that position without causing damage to something, because you probably can't. However, it is a movement that your body would benefit from if you *could* get there and there will be a step-by-step approach to your future squatting self in Chapter 7. The point now is to understand that your body should be able to get into this position and what a healthy position it is for your hips and pelvis.

As riders, it is an important consideration. The muscular activity required to lower into and move out of a deep squat, the mobility required in the hips and ankles and the alignment of the pelvis and lower back all make it a key posture for building strength and flexibility throughout the body that can prepare it for sitting in the saddle incredibly well.

A full, deep squat was a natural movement for your ancestors. It is excellent for hip, pelvic, ankle and lower back health.

TONE VS TENSION

Good muscle tone refers to a muscle that works with the right amount of strength at the right time and for the right duration. This occurs when muscles are able to 'fire' correctly, allowing them to contract and then return to their optimal length.

A tense muscle is only able to sit in one position: one that is too taut. It is unable to release back to its optimal length. This disables movement and compromises function.

THE GLUTE AND SACROILIAC JOINT CONNECTION

The sacroiliac joint occurs where the bones of the pelvis (ilia) 'meet' the sacrum via strong ligament attachments, so the sacrum 'floats' between the two main bones of the pelvis. The ligament attachment helps to increase the space within the pelvic cavity by lifting the sacrum away from the ilia when the body is in a deep squat, as this was the position traditionally adopted for childbirth and toileting. This movement capability and the relatively unstable nature of the attachment are managed through muscular support when the leg is pulled behind the body by the glutes and the leg is loaded. Activation of the glutes removes most of the movement potential of the sacrum so that force can be transferred between the trunk, pelvis and legs. Once again, this firing of the glutes and subsequent sacroiliac joint support can only occur if the hip is able to be moved into extension. For the rider, keeping this joint healthy on the ground is essential to avoid any instability in the saddle as it has to absorb the loads created by the horse's hind limbs.

FORM DICTATES FUNCTION

The position (and therefore form) of the parts of your body determines how they can and will be used (their function).

The hip, knee, foot connection

The hip, knee and foot work together in a kinetic chain that sends communications both ways. It is a bit of a 'to me, to you' kind of scenario, as the way the foot interacts with the ground will affect the position of the knee and the hip, and similarly the way the hip sits in the joint, how it moves and how strong the muscles are around it, will affect the shape of the foot and therefore how the foot is able to interact with the ground. How your knees and feet travel, whether they point straight, turn out or face towards each other, develops tension in the muscular chains of the entire leg from hip to foot. These tensions will affect how you are able to position your leg in the saddle and will contribute to whether your toes point out, or if you get cramp in your hips, or grip with your knees (*see* Chapter 4).

Your body was built to have consistent interaction with the ground through feet that were unencumbered by footwear. This kept the foot aligned and strong, which (through muscular and fascial connections) supported the knee to stay facing forwards. The hips were attached to a pelvis that was consistently moved in a way that kept the hip joints not just mobile but strong in terms of muscular health all around the joint – front, sides and back. This strength was built from keeping the head of the femur (the ball part of the hip joint) facing forwards rather than rotating inwards towards the ilium or rotating externally. The femur connects with the bones of the knee joint, which connect to the shin. These then connect to the bones in the foot. All the way along there are soft tissues responding to these connections, and therefore whatever happens at the hip will affect the shape of the foot and vice versa. Any deviation in walking that doesn't have the foot and knee pointing straight ahead places tensions on the muscles that affect the hip. A foot that turns outwards, for example, pulls the hip into a position of constant external rotation, which means the joint space between the femur and the acetabulum is reduced. Loading the leg in this position will create heat, friction and ultimately a wearing away of the hip joint (osteoarthritis).

The knees (as a close relative to the pelvis and hips)

The knees are the meeting point of the way the foot interacts with the ground (forces from the bottom) and the way the hips and pelvis are functioning (forces from above). As the centre point of these forces, the knees are vulnerable to weaknesses from both ends. Walking, as we have seen, is a fundamental movement for the human body but to make sure we have coloured the whole picture in, it is necessary to address the *way* in which the body walks. Not all movement is created equal and the position the body is designed to be in when walking is with the feet pointing straight ahead, like the tyres on a car going in a straight line. A child born 200,000 years ago would have learned to walk a lot earlier than the children of today. They did not wear shoes, nor did they waddle around in nappies. They would not have been placed in a chair to eat or to learn or to be transported. They would have squatted, exercised their feet over different terrain, been carried by parents and explored moving their body for most of the day. At five years old their movement education would have continued, unlike children of modern society at the same age who have to attend school and sit in chairs for most of the day. This all added up to strong muscular support of the pelvis and hips, and their feet would have been able to signal to the brain where the body was in time and space. This movement would have been continuous. As the body grew older and stronger, more movement would have taken place. Outsourcing the resisting of gravity to chairs would not have happened and no other movement constrictions would

RIDING AND EXTERNAL ROTATION OF THE HIPS

Riding requires that the hips move into external rotation. This means that the femur is turned outwards. This requires the action of a small but very strong muscle known as the piriformis, located deep within the buttocks. This muscle is notoriously tight in horse riders, as it is asked to maintain the hips in this external rotation for the duration the rider is in the saddle. Excess shortening of this muscle can be the cause of sciatic pain, hip pain and lower back pain. The tension of this muscle is exacerbated through poor alignment patterns on the ground; knees that knock together and feet which point out like a duck's will place this muscle under tension. When you come to ride with a tight, weak muscle that is required to contract and work for an hour or more it becomes irritated and inflamed. This response can then create friction against the close-lying sciatic nerve. The question now is whether riding is causing the problem with your hips, or is it the hips you turn up to ride with that are the problem?

have been imposed. As a result, the body developed strength from a place of alignment, which included walking with the feet pointing straight ahead.

OSTEOARTHRITIS

Osteoarthritis, a Greek word meaning inflammation of the bone and joint (osteo meaning 'of the bone', arthr 'of the joint' and itis 'inflammation'), is the break-down of joint cartilage and bone, causing stiffness, reduced mobility and pain. It is not a disease, but a condition that occurs because loads on the joints have been too great, or applied from the wrong position, and the bones have rubbed constantly against one another. Rubbing between two surfaces creates friction, and friction creates heat. It is this heat that is the source of the damaging inflammation of the joint.

The anatomy

The knee is a hinge joint. This means it should bend and extend to enable us to walk with a smooth gait. There is naturally some weight-bearing and force resistance to gravity but its main function is as a locomotive joint.

To fulfil its role, the knee is cushioned with cartilage and has a full ligament support system (front, back, sides). Any shearing or torque of the bones of the knee joint (i.e. sliding inwards) creates too much stress on the ligaments that are designed to keep the bones on top of each other, in alignment. If you walk with your upper body tipping forwards, you are loading the cartilage and ligaments of your knees rather than the weight-bearing bones of your legs. This means that the cartilage of the knees has to behave like a crash mat by catching your falling upper body. Over time,

the cartilage wears away and the bones begin to crash into each other with no protection.

The feet and ankles

The foot itself is made up of twenty-six bones, thirty-three joints and a matrix of more than a hundred soft tissues. It is designed for a

BENDING, LIFTING AND THE KNEES

Bending the knees, not the back, when lifting heavy items became the narrative that society believed and obediently followed in an attempt to save the ever-increasing burden of lower back pain. This message wasn't entirely incorrect: indeed, it is important to avoid flexing the spine under load, but this message simply transferred the weakness in the lower back to a wearing-out of the knees. The knees are predominantly a hinge joint. They do have more movement than pure flexion and extension, but their function in the body is not to take large amounts of load, and when they do take some load under flexion, they should always stay in line with the ankles to avoid too much pressure being placed on the joint capsule. The instruction to 'bend from the knees to lift loads' meant that people started loading their knees from a flexed position that travelled over their toes. In this position the joint receives severe compression forces which can damage cartilage and stress the positioning of the bones. A better way to lift is from the hips, utilizing the back of the body as it was intended: to be strong in raising the upper body, and keep the knees over the ankles so they are not moved to the end range of their capability and then have to take load. This is demonstrated in Chapter 7.

complex mix of movement, information gathering, stability and force dampening (via the ankle). As with the rest of the body, the foot has not changed in design since our early ancestors became bipeds. In those days, the foot would have met the earth with either no barrier (bare foot) or with a thin animal skin strapped onto it. Consistently loading the foot without any barrier to its interaction with the ground ensured that it developed as strong, wide and dextrous. In this manner it operated as a highly intelligent infantry officer. It was on the front line, strong in holding position but also constantly delivering intelligence back to headquarters: the central nervous system. It is a fine piece of engineering. Interacting with the ground in this way enabled the joints to be mobile enough to move over, bend and wrap around different terrain. The sophisticated network of proprioceptors was awake and alert, constantly communicating with the brain on the body's position in time and space. This melody of movement from the foot would have created an environment in which the ankle was strong enough to adjust, correct its positioning and protect the rest of the limb from movement that could take the other joints of the limb out of alignment.

Walking and the upper body

As walking was such a repetitive, consistent and integral part of life for the newly evolved human, the shape of the body which took each step was fundamental to how strong, mobile, pain-free and injury-resistant that body was going to be. Pelvic positioning, as discussed, needed to be in neutral for hip mobility and pelvic strength, but the position of the upper body also played a significant role in how the body was loaded. Walking from a vertically aligned position ensured that the shoulders stayed over the ribs, which stayed over the hips. This ensured that the upper body remained upright and tall (important for the mechanic of breathing) and it also meant that the arms and shoulder joints had the

WALKING, THE TREADMILL AND YOU

Walking across the ground builds strength at the back of the body because of the law of physics that says in order to move forward, you must first push back. This action requires the glutes and hamstrings to activate, which stabilizes and builds a strong environment for the pelvis and lumbar spine. Walking on the treadmill, although it appears to be exactly the same, requires a completely different mechanic. The moving belt takes the leg behind the body, so the muscles at the back of the leg don't have anything to do. Instead, the muscles at the front of the leg – the hip flexors – have to contract to lift the limb and pull it forwards. Shortening these muscles leaves the body vulnerable to lower back, hip and knee dysfunction, particularly when their action is not leveraged against any contraction of the glutes. The belt itself also does not provide the body with any variance in terrain, so the foot and ankle are not preparing for life outside.

If you have ever trained for distance running on the treadmill for an outside event, you may have been surprised that you found it easier to run further on the treadmill. This is because, on the belt, you are using less muscular activity to reach the required distance. The same applies to treadmills used for horses. They can be extremely useful in controlling stride symmetry and length, but they should not be used with an expectation to build strength in the muscles that push the horse across the ground.

best range of movement. A naturally evolved mechanic of walking is to swing the arms in diagonal reciprocation to the movement of the legs. When the leg is moved behind the body it creates a twist through the pelvis and spine. If this were done for ten to twelve miles every day, the tension through the lower back would be too great and the intervertebral discs would be at risk of damage from vertebral torque. To counteract the twist, the arms swing in the opposite direction and by doing so they apply enough load to keep the lower back straight and reduce torque through the spine. This action also tones the triceps at the back of the arms. Walking without swinging your arms feels very odd, because it is a fundamental, instinctive response from the body: a true, undeniable feature of a body that knows exactly how it should be moving.

THE SPINE

The human spine consists of thirty-three vertebrae, which are organized into segments. Each segment has its own architecture, which arose from movement protocols the body was expected to carry out. Understanding the spine is useful for every human, but particularly for those who want to ride. Spinal health impacts the whole of the body and a weak, poorly supported vertebral column will impact everything you do with your horse, both on and off his back.

The vertebrae are separated by thick, fibrous structures known as discs, whose purpose is to provide shock absorption and to allow the vertebrae to move with protection from bone-on-bone friction. The spine is not a self-supporting structure; it relies on an array of muscles, ligaments and fascia to keep it upright but with this help it gives the body shape, allows the body to stand upright and provides the spinal cord with a safe place to travel through. The spinal cord is the transmitter of

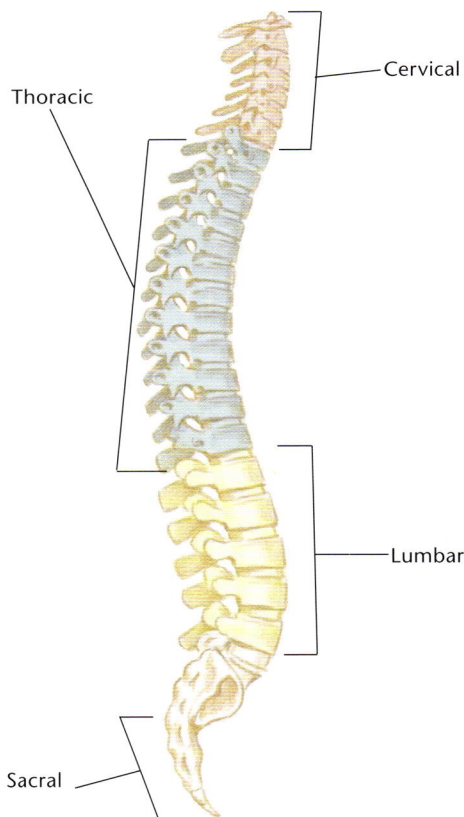

Fig. 16 The spine is arranged into curves to allow movement and to help transmit concussion. It is at its most healthy when it forms the shape of a shallow 'S'

information from the brain to the rest of the body, with spinal nerves coming from it to service each area of the body. The cord itself runs from the brain stem at the top of the spine and travels down to the first and second lumbar vertebrae, from where it continues as a bundle of nerves known as the 'cauda equina' or horse's tail. The spine itself ends just after the cauda equina, which is what makes lumbar punctures and epidurals possible without directly affecting the spinal cord itself.

The curves of the spine show a very shallow 'S' shape, forming a balance of curvature that helps to provide strength and stability to the body whilst making possible a wide array of movement. It is these curves that the natural movement protocols of our forefathers maintained, which ensured that the spaces between the vertebrae stayed at a healthy level. Problems arise when the vertebrae are either forced out of these curves or the curves become too exaggerated. In either scenario the discs are placed under too much stress from vertebrae closing in on one another.

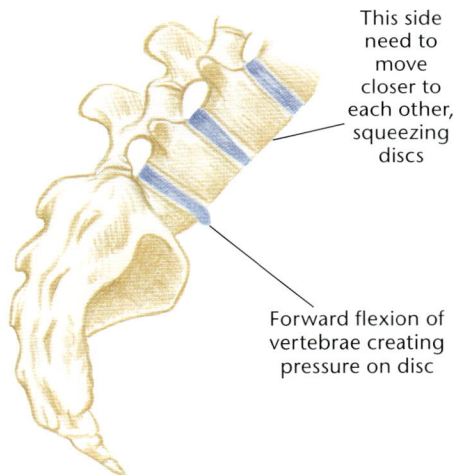

This side need to move closer to each other, squeezing discs

Forward flexion of vertebrae creating pressure on disc

Fig. 17   When the spine is constantly asked to move into flexion, the intervertebral discs can receive too much pressure, causing them to bulge or leak.

THE UPPER BODY

The design of the upper body is based around the housing protecting the vital organs the heart and lungs. The protective cavity of the rib-cage creates a chamber for the lungs to expand into, as does the curve of the spine which faces away from the body. This design ensures that the lungs and ribs can fully expand during inhalation, which provides the body with maximal oxygen; on a biomechanical level it also provides the

FASCIA

The fascia is a web of connective tissue that covers each and every muscle individually, as well as wrapping the entire muscular system as a whole. It is this mass of connections that explains how problems in the jaw can affect the hip, or how the feet can affect the shoulders. The body is designed to work as independent parts coming together to service the whole, but ultimately each part is co-dependent on each and every other part doing its job.

Fascia can become incredibly tight and dehydrated, and because it acts as a protective sleeve around each muscle, the amount of movement it has – or doesn't have – will dictate the amount of muscular activity that can occur. Fascia can help you to understand why small, seemingly insignificant adjustments to the body can have a huge impact on its overall biomechanic health. When one area of the body is moved, it exerts a tug on this web of connective tissue, which can affect an area of the body quite distant from the original load.

torso with strength and support. When the ribs are fully expanded the limbs can work independently from the body and the spine is fully supported. It is a feature that developed through the need for cardiovascular endurance whilst moving the body over uneven or challenging terrain. Knowing how to breathe correctly was a key feature of letting the body work as well as it needed to through times of physical stress.

The thoracic vertebrae rely upon muscular support to keep them upright and stacked on top of each other correctly. The muscles that maintain their positioning are strengthened through the position of the arms, the activity of the shoulders and the position of the head relative to the vertebrae. Again, alignment matters. Maintaining a posture that is able to resist gravity is the dream of the upper body, and it can only do this if the shoulders are positioned over the hips. The arms are not part of the postural support system for the body, but they do create positional drag on the shoulders, neck and muscles of the upper body because of the way they are connected. This means they can affect posture, even if they are not directly responsible for it. The arm attaches to the body via the scapula (shoulder blade), a broad, wing-shaped bone that is attached to the thoracic vertebrae via muscles. The shoulder joint, the scapula and its connection to the spine together create the *shoulder girdle*, a trio of parts that work together. Because of this connection, any movements the arms make and the position they are held in will affect the shape of the thoracic spine. In the good old days the arms would have been used for carrying, pushing things away from the body and pulling the body towards the hands. They would have been regularly dealing with loads from a variety of different directions, which all served to strengthen the attachment of the scapula to the body. By keeping these vertebrae/scapula muscles strong, the upper body was well supported to maintain an upright position that could be loaded over the hips and not succumb to the pull of gravity.

THE LUMBAR SPINE

The lower back consists of six vertebrae that are designed to be the strut of connection from the pelvis to the rib-cage. It is capable of forward flexion, side bending and extension but most of the rotation of the spine occurs in the thoracic vertebrae above it.

The lumbar vertebrae are supported by an army of muscles that are responsible for stabilizing the spine and allowing movement and mobility through the waist.

THE TRUTH ABOUT THE CORE

The core should be thought of as every muscle that attaches to the pelvis (of which there are over thirty), the hips, the thighs, the bottom ribs and the lumbar vertebrae. The core is the area that relates to the area from the bottom of the ribs to the top of the thighs – front, back, sides, top and bottom. It is a cylinder of muscular layers loaded at the top by a three-dimensional cage (ribs) and sitting on top of

RIDING AND ALIGNMENT

Riding is a sport of alignment; how the rider's body stacks up in the saddle relative to itself and to the horse is at the heart of every positional correction. The alignment protocol of the classical rider's seat arose from the need to place the rider in the most balanced position to allow the horse to move confidently and with minimal stress/overload to the limbs. The whole premise of riding is centred on horse and rider moving in balance with each other. At the core of balance is *alignment*. If horse and/or rider are not in alignment within themselves or with each other, they cannot be balanced.

The horse also has to be aligned if he is going to maintain balance underneath a rider, but his alignment is on a horizontal plane. This means that in order for his body to distribute weight evenly between left and right sides for strength, mobility and balanced, efficient, pain-free movement, his shoulders must be in front of his hindquarters and his head and neck must be in the centre of his chest.

another three-dimensional cage (the pelvis). The only bony component of the main section are the vertebrae of the lumbar spine. This means that this mid-section of the body is designed for *movement*, both to facilitate it and to absorb it. The muscles of the core vary in strength, make-up, length and function but they all share a common theme: they all behave as the switchboard of movement to the body, recognizing and dealing with the activity of the limbs and spine and deciding on how to respond to maintain equilibrium within the body.

The muscles of the core are a diverse team. Some support the spine when you cough or sneeze or laugh, some switch on when you walk, and others come on when you run or sing. They allow the waist to twist, bend forwards and sideways, and extend. The diaphragm at the top enables you to breathe and the pelvic floor at the bottom stops your organs from falling out of your body.

As the only bony (and therefore form-providing) portion of the core, the lumbar vertebrae are a supportive strut connecting the rib-cage to the pelvis to prevent the entire mid-section from collapsing. This strut transmits force and provides resistance against gravity, and as such provides guidelines for the overall movement possibilities of this predominantly muscular section. Without any other bony structure to give the lumbar spine support, its integrity in terms of positioning and therefore health relies solely on the strength and activity of the muscles that connect to it.

vertebrae to each other. Each multifidus spans three joints and creates a scaffolding of strength for the back. These muscles are highly innervated, which means they are designed to respond rapidly to movement stimulus, helping them to activate and therefore support the spine before motion takes place. Poor movement protocols can switch these muscles off (*see* Chapter 3).

The erector spinae muscles are long and broad and have strong fascial connections along the length of the spine. They enable the larger movements of the spine: extension, lateral bending and rotation.

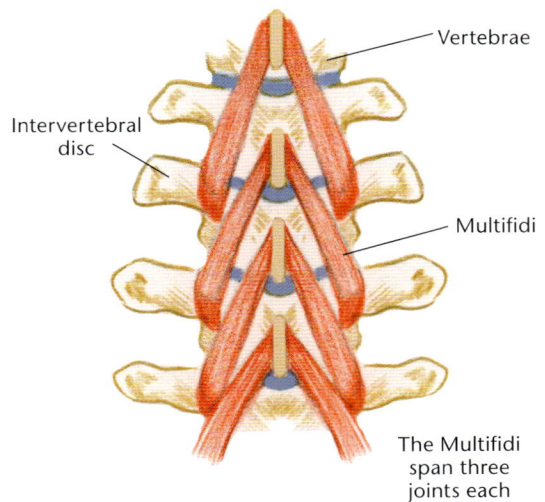

*Fig. 18 **The multifidi muscles; these deep vertebrae stabilizers cross three joints and provide scaffolding for the spine.***

THE MUSCLES OF THE LOWER BACK

The multifidi

At the deepest level are the short and powerful multifidi, which connect the

The quadratus lumborum connects the ribs to the top of the pelvis, so its health is directly affected by the position of the pelvis and how it relates to the position of the rib-cage. This muscle provides right and left side bending and helps to stabilize the lumbar spine/pelvic connection.

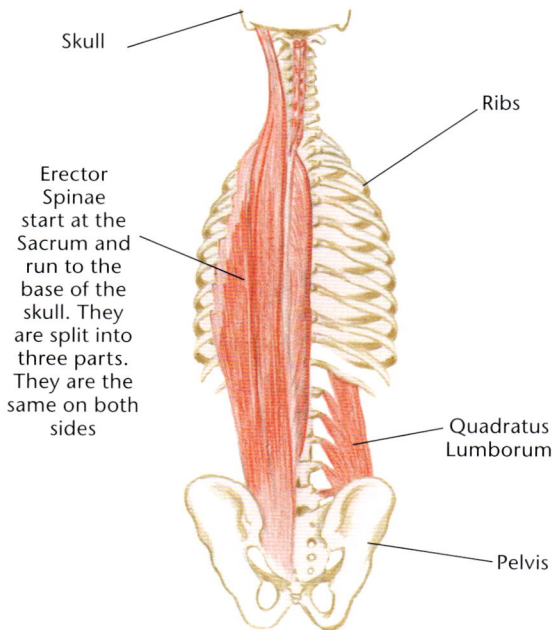

Skull

Ribs

Erector Spinae start at the Sacrum and run to the base of the skull. They are split into three parts. They are the same on both sides

Quadratus Lumborum

Pelvis

Fig. 19   The erector spinae and quadratus lumborum muscles. The erector spinae muscles run from the sacrum all the way to the skull and provide strong spinal support, helping to hold it in an upright position. The quadratus lumborum muscle attaches to the top of the pelvis, the lumbar vertebrae and the bottom rib, and enables sideways flexion and is an important part of the lower back strength network.

muscles (known as the six pack), which run the length from ribs to pelvis and enable the spine to flex. Around the sides are the oblique muscles, enabling side bending and rotating, and at the deepest level is the corset-style muscle, the transverse abdominus. This is a larger muscle that has attachments to the linea alba, the pelvis and the vertebrae, and plays a major role in how strong the core can be as it responds to the position of the lumbar spine.

As a rule, muscles require something solid (bone) to attach to in order to generate force. In the case of the muscles of the front and sides of the core, they have limited anchor points in the form of bones to create an attachment to. To get around this slight inconvenience, the muscles create a spider's web arrangement from their tendons, which weave and interlock together. This means that any movement, anywhere in the body, that directs a pull onto one side of the core will have an effect on the whole area. This helps to explain why core strength is a whole body conversation as opposed to being about isolated movements.

THE FRONT AND SIDES OF THE CORE

The muscles of the lower back may well be the leaders of core health, but the muscles at the front and sides of the core still have a significant role to play in core strength and whole body function.

Running down the centre of the core, from the sternum to the pelvis, is a strong ligament known as the linea alba. Either side of this are the rectus abdominus

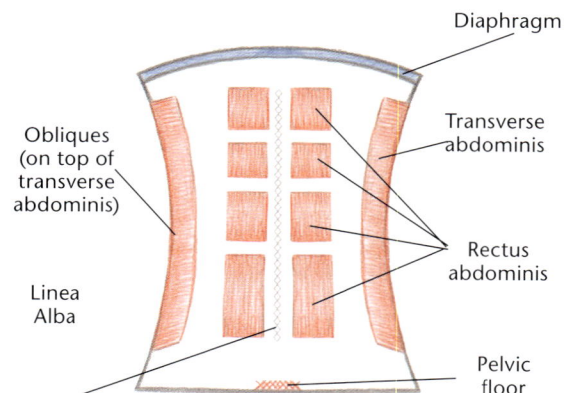

Diaphragm

Obliques (on top of transverse abdominis)

Transverse abdominis

Rectus abdominis

Linea Alba

Pelvic floor

Fig. 20   The muscles of the front of the core which are responsible for switching on at the level needed for the activity the body is doing.

THE DIAPHRAGM

The diaphragm sits below the rib-cage and acts as a muscular lid to the core, whilst also separating the thorax and the abdomen. It is a dome-shaped muscle that attaches to the sternum, the last six ribs and the lumbar vertebrae. It is the chief respiratory muscle, providing mechanical support to the process of inhalation and exhalation through its effect on the rib-cage. When in a relaxed state it sits in a soft, upward curve. During inhalation, the muscles between the ribs (intercostals) move the ribs apart and the diaphragm flattens as the ribs expand. This flattening increases the space within the thorax for the lungs to expand into, and it also reduces the pressure so the lungs are drawn downwards. The intention of the entire breathing apparatus is to maintain the expansion experienced when the diaphragm is flat and the ribs are fully widened and lifted, as it is in this position that the torso and spine are the most supported and limb movement can be the most independent. Diaphragm strength was designed to be maintained through a body moving in a place of vertical alignment, which critically enabled the front of the body to be tall and open. This opening of the chest allowed for the greatest level of expansion to get as much oxygen into the body as possible – a key feature for the hunter-gatherer lifestyle which relied on cell endurance. (Correct breathing technique and how it can help your riding is covered in Chapter 6.)

The 'core of the body' – i.e. the area from diaphragm to pelvic floor and everything in-between – was engineered for dynamic stability: the ability to be secure whilst on the move. In order to achieve this, the muscles of the core had to have strength, tone and the ability to respond to reflex.

Strengthening of the core in bygone eras was not done through a hundred sit-ups a day or three-minute planks or side crunches. The body evolved to thrive from movement, and as the body moved so the core was strengthened.

The muscles of the core activate when the rest of your body does something. If you lift your arms above your head, bend your knees, walk, jump, stand up from sitting, sit down, laugh or sing, your core will respond. It is also designed to switch on for biological functions such as coughing, vomiting and toileting. The whole premise of muscular performance is that the muscles switch on at the level required for the activity they are being asked to do. It is no different for the muscles of the core. Where they do differ is *how* they are asked to switch on. For most muscular activity, you are probably used to creating an obvious movement, which then activates the muscle responsible to kick into gear (think of a bicep curl), but the muscles of the core were designed to respond to a reflex created by movement potential rather than from a conscious activation by you.

So what does this mean?

Every movement the body makes affects the trunk. Moving from a place of alignment, as the body was designed to do, ensured that the right joints received the right loads and therefore the correct signals were sent to the stabilizing centre of the core. The body became a vehicle of dynamic stillness, with the ability to choose the position it wanted regardless of the surface it was standing or sitting on. This is an inbuilt proprioceptive system that we still possess today. Every human body has the ability to self-organize itself in time and space according to what action the limbs and spine are required to do. The reflex action of the core muscles should begin with the multifidi, which are highly sensitive to movement. These short, strong muscles are responsible for keeping the vertebrae stabilized to deal with loads so when the limbs initiate movement, these muscles are designed to switch on at the appropriate level. This reflex response then guides the reaction of the larger, more superficial muscles of the lower back to activate. As a unit, the muscles at the sides, bottom and front of the core then switch on as necessary. This is the natural reflex response of the core. The movement environment for the human body was designed to ensure the limbs, trunk, pelvis and spine were moved in various ways for a lot of the day. Like anything that has to work a lot, they become strong and well practised in their role. This constant variety of movement kept the multifidi strong, alert and incredibly responsive.

The idea that the core needs to be held in a static state is a symptom of modern movement behaviours and lower back problems (*see* Chapter 3). Common instructions include pulling the tummy button towards the spine and actively lifting the pelvic floor to prepare the body for any movement that involves the spine. This idea buys into the myth that muscular tension is the same as muscular strength, but, as we saw in Chapter 1, in order to be strong, a muscle has to be able to contract and relax back to its optimal length. This provides tone, which is functional, whereas tension inhibits movement. By holding the core in a static position the muscles are unable to respond to any of the reflex signals they might be receiving. In effect, you are binding the muscles to a level of tension that you have deemed appropriate for the movement you are about to do. The idea of sucking the tummy button in and 'engaging' the core arose as a result of the epidemic of chronic lower back pain. The aim of instructing people to engage their core artificially was in an attempt to protect the weak and vulnerable lumbar spine. This also goes together with the idea of sit-ups being the answer to strengthening the core, by making the front of the body the area of most significance, as opposed to the back, without realizing that

the very action of a sit-up serves to weaken the lower back even more.

The human body is truly a mechanical masterpiece. It flourished in the environment for which it evolved, and targeted core strength was not on its daily to-do list. It was an automatic response from aligned, varied movement that kept the back of the body strong and the front of the body tall and open.

ATTENDING TO THE DETAIL

It is not enough to consider your body as a single unit. In reality, it is a unit made up of many different parts, all of which need to be kept alive and healthy through the movement they were designed to do. It is the small, intentional, regular movements of each smaller part that have the biggest impact on the whole.

SYMMETRY AND POSTURAL SLINGS: A NOTE

As the entire body is connected through a web of fascia, the movement and loading of muscles in one area will influence the health of muscles in other areas. These postural slings behave as a line of 'pull', so they contour to the body in fluid lines either vertically, horizontally or diagonally.

The relevance of knowing about these comes down to symmetry, which is a key part of any rider's repertoire. Natural movement demanded that the body was used in all planes of motion. People would still have had a dominant hand, but the impact on the body would have been minimized through more tasks that required both arms and jobs that needed whole body involvement.

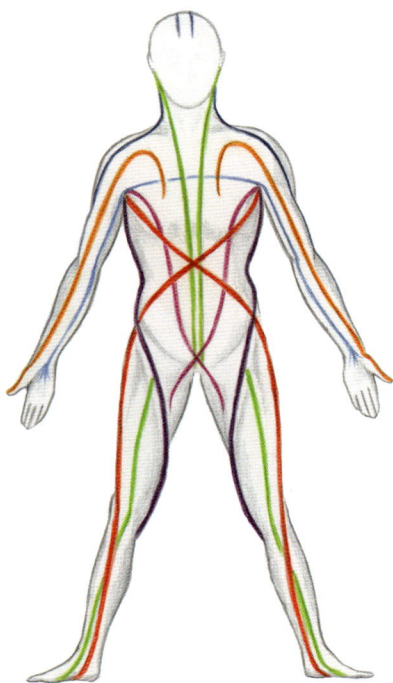

Fig. 21   The body is a network of muscular slings that connect vertically, horizontally and diagonally across the body. This explains how each section of the body can affect the function of another.

The dominance of one hand over the other means that you will likely make more movements with just one arm. From grooming your horse to picking items from the supermarket shelf, the chances are it is your dominant hand in action.

SYMMETRY

A human body, like that of a horse, will never be fully symmetrical. The aim should always be to minimize the effect of any asymmetric tendencies through the body, which means using the postural slings as evenly and as often as possible.

RIDING WITH YOUR ANCESTOR'S BODY

If your body was habitually used in this way, sitting in a saddle would still be abnormal for it, but it would be naturally able to adopt better alignment and have the length through the torso, the strength at the back of the body and good mobility through the hips and ankles so that a balanced position that moved with the horse wouldn't be too hard to attain. The core would be strong from being moved in all directions and your postural slings (i.e. connections and tractions across the body) would be far more symmetrical.

This builds more tension in some postural slings than others, creating an imbalance and taking the body further away from symmetry.

To summarize, your body wants:

- a long open chest and torso (front of the body);
- a strong posterior chain (lower back, glutes, hamstrings);
- hips that are the fulcrum for the body and can move into full extension;
- ribs that fully expand with each breath;
- hips that are loaded with the body's weight;
- hips, knees and ankles that are strong and flexible, able to complete their full range of movement whilst maintaining their integrity and allowing the body to sink into a full squat;
- knees that allow the leg to bend and move the body smoothly across the ground;
- feet that are wide and dextrous and which point straight ahead; and
- arms and shoulders that can pull the body towards them and push things away from the body.

3 Your Movement Lifestyle and the Shape of Your Body

If someone asked you about the environment you live in, you would possibly describe how many neighbours you have, what your garden looks like or how close the shops are. If you were asked about the environment your horse lives in, you might describe the stable or the paddock and how often you ride. So what might you say if you were asked about your *movement* environment? When, during the day, are you moving your body? When are you moving your body differently? And how long are you moving your body for? Your lifestyle may be centred around the activities you do, your job, your family, your horse. Each day is probably a whirlwind of activity, rushing from one priority to the next and pausing only to grab a coffee. Hopefully, your body allows you to get through the day; maybe with a few niggles and some stiffness, but generally it doesn't stop you achieving what you need to so you don't really have to give it much thought. Until you do. Until you can't turn your head to reverse the car, or you can't stand upright because your lower back is too painful, or your hips need a few steps to get moving when you get out of the car. Your movement lifestyle, which is the amount and type of movement your body does all the time, will determine how it functions, the amount of pain it gives you, whether or not you will need to visit the surgeon or how often you require the chiropractor/osteopath/massage therapist/physiotherapist. Your movement habits are displayed in the shape of your body,

as is your awareness of them, just as they are displayed in your position in the saddle. Learning how to move may seem like another chore on your never-ending to-do list, but you are moving anyway. You are in your body all the time. Knowing how your movement lifestyle is impacting the shape of your body is critical if you want to be a rider who can move themselves and their horse away from pain and towards sound and sustainable performance.

Your body is a machine that has been around for hundreds of thousands of years but is now required to live in a very different way from that for which it evolved. The landscape of modern society has outmanoeuvred human physiology. The arrival of agriculture, industry and technology has happened, in relative terms, incredibly rapidly – too rapidly for the ancient machine of the human body to adapt sufficiently to the positions and 'environment' it is now required to live within. There quite simply hasn't been enough time for evolution to transition the body into something that is more suited to the way it is now used. The modern environment has been created for convenience; from grocery deliveries, public transport and furniture, to computerized homes, society has very successfully removed the need for physical activity. How people move on a global scale connects cultures in a way that is more cohesive than habits of shopping, eating or voting and this is confirmed by the sheer number of people suffering with crippling pain or obesity, and requiring surgery and joint replacements. These experiences of chronic suffering have become the normal landscape for our culture and one that is expected and commonly accepted.

In light of this, you would be forgiven for believing that the human body is flawed, that it is riddled with design faults that all lead to an inevitable, shuffling demise as your years advance. The narrative of this inevitability of pain, lack of movement, crumbling bones and clogged arteries has become an unchallenged blueprint in societies' collective consciousness. For riders, this belief drives a fear and sense of scarcity of time left in the saddle because of a current sore hip and a grumbling lower back. This belief – that the activities you enjoy doing will be curtailed by a body unwilling to keep going – reduces your power to do anything about it. But does it really have to be the beginning of the end? Are you really in a body whose prime intention is to let you down and cripple you with pain? What if there was nothing wrong with this remarkable system but rather that the system is being used incorrectly? You know that the body you are in was built for movement: regular and varied movement carried out from a place of alignment. By looking at your movement environment you should be able to start painting a picture of how much – or how little – you move your body, how much of your body is being moved at any one time and from what position this movement is occurring.

On the surface of things you might have an acceptable, if not above average, level of movement in your life. Maybe you walk the dog, deal with the horse, run around after children, tend to the garden, ride, take a fitness class, swim or jog, go to the gym. Maybe you walk or cycle to work and go hiking at the weekends. You may well live within an environment that appears quite active; if so, this is great. But not all movement is created equal, so it is necessary to take a look at what position your body is doing these activities in.

There will undoubtedly be some time in a car or on a train as you commute to work, there will be time spent sitting at a desk or perhaps in some other static or repetitive posture. If you have to stand for long periods of time, or you are riding eight horses a day, these are both activities which might be 'better' or higher on a linear scale than sitting down, but they still restrict the amount and variety of movement that the body will do. Professional riders riding all day still suffer with back pain and demonstrate some level of biomechanic dysfunction as their bodies are in a place of repetitive geometry, so it is more about the type and variety of positions you put your body in that is going to keep it healthy.

It is likely that for most of the day you will be wearing some form of footwear and most of your walking will be on reasonably safe, level surfaces. You will sit on comfortable furniture and sleep on a mattress that contours to your body. As well as these movements all being part of your day, the other piece of the story is that you will perform all your daily movements in exactly the same way. You will get dressed, brush your teeth, make breakfast, sit on the same chair, drive the car, do the horse chores and ride all in the same way. These repetitive patterns have provided you with the current shape of your body and, in a chicken and egg scenario, this shape will then dictate how you move. These movement habits typically create a body that has movement limitations, excess muscular tension, muscular imbalances, loading patterns and sequences of use that remove fundamental levels of mobility in some or many of your joints and soft tissues. For a while, you will continue asking the same things of your body, unaware of the dysfunction that is building. This scenario cannot last for ever, and at some point the body will stop regenerating cells, muscles will become shorter or longer on a cellular level (*see* Chapter 1) and you may experience some sort of injury. More time will pass until your horse decides to make an unrequired movement on the end of the lead and pulls your arm, or you trip up a kerb or you bend down to pick feet out and cannot stand upright again because your lower back won't let you. Your movement becomes even less as you nurse the injury and your movement lifestyle deteriorates even further. Awareness of what your body is doing usually doesn't occur until it shouts loudly enough through pain for some attention. By this point, damage has already occurred and the climb out of the valley is steep and enduring. By knowing how your body wants to move (*see* Chapter 2) and being aware of how modern life takes it away from this place, you can begin to make adjustments that use the system correctly, so that the crash doesn't have to happen.

HOW IS EXERCISE SERVING YOU?

We are certainly living in an era of 'exercise'. Gyms, fitness classes, online workouts, yoga, pilates, cross fit, zumba: the list goes on. There seems to be an endless array of ways to exercise and you can choose one that benefits you on the most levels; are you looking for a social hour, a bit of joy dancing to some fun tunes, maybe you need to relax the mind, or you want to be specific and hit the pilates equipment. There is no doubt that exercise is good for you but the way it is being done – or more specifically the body it is being done from – may mean that it is not serving every bit of you in the best way. This is in no way suggesting that you shouldn't exercise, but rather a pointer towards understanding that your body needs a foundation of alignment and function, so whatever exercise you want to add on top of that, for whatever motivation, you are doing it from a strong and stable base. Adding load to an unbalanced structure is a surefire way to weaken it until it breaks down, so all the movement you do is more

beneficial if it is done with an awareness of how it is helping you, or *if* it is in fact helping you. Some things you do might be detrimental for where your body is at; certainly, loading a dysfunction with weight or impact or speed will increase the risk of injury. This can mean that your endeavours of working out to get stronger actually mean that you are adding to the pile of debris within your tissues, creating the perfect habitat for pain and injury. Many gym-goers can be heard lamenting about why they are the ones plagued with injury when they are trying to look after themselves ('I never hurt this much or had as many injuries before I started going to the gym'); well, no, because injury (when it is not caused by direct trauma) occurs when you move or load more of the body than you are used to. From shin splints to rotator cuff problems, a programme of 'lack of use' quickly becomes a programme of 'over use' when you start putting mechanical loads on areas of the body that have not been used and where cell health is not viable (*see* Chapter 1). Outsourcing movement the way culture dictates leaves the body vulnerable to movement stressors because of muscle imbalances, immobility and pain. It also leaves you with a body in a shape that is unable to cope with new movements (or loads) when they do show up in front of you, like moving something heavy out of the way and 'putting your back out'. The amount and type of movement you provide your body can set you up for the ailments you might consider to be out of our control: hereditary, bad luck or circumstantial. However, the way you stand, sit, walk and sleep writes a much more powerful story over the condition and health of your body than genes or ageing ever could.

SPINAL DECOMPRESSION

Your spine is the channel of communication with your brain on everything related to movement for your entire body. It is your structural support, it gives you shape and it provides attachments for muscles and bones so that your body can move as a holistic unit. As a communication channel, it houses the spinal cord, which runs from the brain stem to the base of the spine. The vertebrae of the spine (through which this magnificent cord runs) are designed to be held in a position where they do not compress onto their neighbour. Each vertebra is separated from its neighbour by a thick, gelatinous disc to prevent any bone on bone contact, but these discs too are designed to be given enough space so they are not deformed or pushed out of place. In order to keep this space between the structures of the spine, and to give the spinal cord a clear channel to pass through, the vertebrae need to be held in a decompressed position. What this points to is that the skull and the tailbone need to be as far away from each other as possible. With a clear channel, messages can flow easily and promptly, enabling effective and efficient communication, which then allows the body to cope with shifting environments. Riding most definitely provides the body with a shifting environment, so having the spine in a healthy state before getting in the saddle helps to prepare the body for all the communications it is going to have to deliver. The problem is that all too often the body is put into positions that fail to maintain this space for the spinal cord. The vertebrae are forced into compression and the discs are placed under so much pressure that they bulge out and interact with the spinal cord, creating acute pain. One of the biggest culprits in creating this environment for the spine is sitting. Collectively, societies are sitting down more now than ever before and it is creating massive health issues in terms of heart disease and obesity. Whilst these are critical conditions to address, my concerns over sitting – from a movement and biomechanical perspective – are due to the shape it puts the body in, and how this impacts the way it can move and, for riders, how it will sit in the saddle.

INTRODUCTION TO THE SITTING CATASTROPHE

As a rider, it is likely that you sit down less than non-riders, but if you have a job that pays for your horse, you may well be sitting at a desk for six to eight hours a day. Add into that some commuting time and some relaxing time at home on the couch, and the hours of sedentary, repetitive posture start to add up. This section is about how sitting changes the shape of your body. On the surface of things you may be wondering why this is relevant to riding, but, as you will discover, the 'chair-friendly' shape your body adopts doesn't leave your body when you stand up – which means it doesn't leave you when you ride, either. Riding with a body that has organized itself into sitting in comfort does not lend itself to attaining the riding position and effectiveness in the saddle that you might be seeking. Sitting down for extended periods of time has been compared to smoking in conversations around cardiovascular health and fitness and a sedentary lifestyle is affecting society's collective waistline and damaging/stressing the nation's heart-beat. This is not untrue, but the story of sitting for prolonged periods of time also forces the body into a shape that takes it as far away from biomechanic excellence as possible, and this is what affects riders more than anything.

The shape you have been creating since you were five years old

Until the age of five, your body would have been developing as close to an optimal 'natural' standard as possible. Close to, but not absolute as you will have worn shoes, been placed in a pushchair, worn nappies and been strapped into other devices to keep you safe. All of these applied some unnatural movement restrictions on your body, but in most cases the time spent before starting school at five years old was largely active: squatting, running, sitting on the floor and climbing, with minimal to no time sitting on furniture. This meant that you used your body as nature intended. However, as soon as you started school you were required to stay in a seated position for five to six hours a day. By the time you were ten, your body (a master adaptor) had set the soft tissues into a position that was chair-friendly, ensuring that sitting down was comfortable and expended the least amount of energy. This is an ancient survival mechanism for the body that dominates many of your movement practices. Your body has a high level of functional tolerance, which means it will adapt to the position it finds itself in most of the time. This is to ensure it doesn't have to expend too much energy, so that when the time comes to move or change what it is doing (such as avoid a predator), it has the energy to do so.

THE MECHANICS OF A BODY IN 'CHAIR SHAPE'

Sitting in a chair for most people is the easiest, most comfortable and comforting position to be in. The body has adapted its musculo-skeletal system for this to be the case. When sitting becomes the activity your body does most of the time, it becomes the shape your body has adapted to all of the time.

What happens to your body: an overview

From a biomechanical perspective your body goes through a cascade of adjustments in order to sit in a chair comfortably.

This functionally changes the entire biomechanical system from one that works to one that starts to crash into itself. The problem with sitting down is not just about the effects of not moving, but what is happening to the body mechanically, because this is what is going to make the difference to your position in the saddle. Riding, at its core, is about mechanics – how the horse moves, how the rider moves, and how the two meet. Knowing how the mechanic of your body is affected by the positions you put it in most of the time allows you to be aware of how you are going to affect the horse's movement, both positively and negatively. When it comes to the mechanic of sitting, it is not just about what happens to your body in the chair. It is about what your chair does to your body – which is different. Sitting is a problem because the shape of the chair doesn't leave your body when you stand up. You may appear to be upright, but appearances can be, and in this case are, deceiving.

The cycle of sitting

- The knees and hips are put into a ninety-degree angle, which reduces the space within the joints and puts pressure on cartilage, connective tissues and blood vessels.
- The glutes become stretched to allow the hips to sit in this position.
- The hip flexors at the front of the hip become shortened and contracted.
- Pressure from the seat on the back of the legs (hamstrings) restricts blood flow to the lower half of the body by as much as 50 per cent after just one hour of sitting.
- The lower back moves into flexion (forward bending), loading the discs and stretching the vertebral stabilizing muscles.
- The pelvis becomes tucked underneath, with most of the weight on the sacrum. This affects the health of the pelvic floor muscles

and interrupts the relationship between the pelvis and lower back.

- The shoulders will move in front of the hips and gravity will start to pull them downwards, increasing the forward curvature of the spine.
- The chin will move away from the neck, adding 4.5kg of extra weight to the top of the spine for every inch the chin moves forward.
- The upper body falling forward collapses the rib-cage, inhibiting the full expansion of the lungs. Subsequent shallow breathing contributes to the shortening of the chest muscles and tension in the muscles of the neck.
- The shoulder joints rotate forwards and inwards towards each other. This weakens the connection of the arms with the body via the scapula to the thoracic vertebrae, as the scapula become lifted and pulled away from the spine.

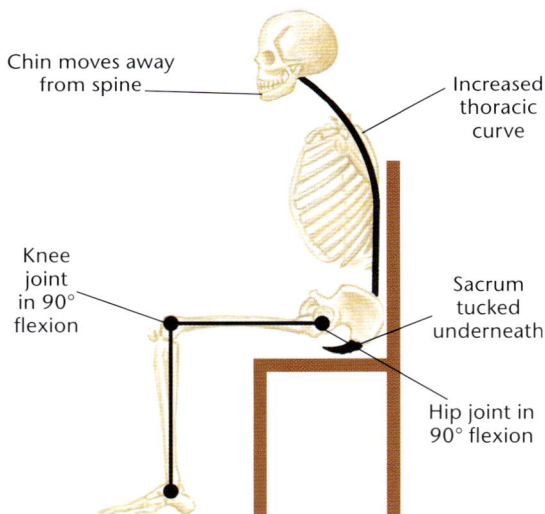

Chin moves away from spine

Increased thoracic curve

Knee joint in 90° flexion

Sacrum tucked underneath

Hip joint in 90° flexion

Fig. 22   Poor sitting posture. The common position that seated posture encourages, demonstrating spinal flexion, pelvic tuck, knees and hips in flexion and the chin moving away from the spine.

These are the adjustments to the system that have to occur when you sit in a chair for any length of time. If you only ever wanted to sit in a chair, this shape, although not ideal, may not cause you too many issues, but if you want to stand up and move and ride, then the impact of the chair on your body is hugely influential.

SITTING AND THE LOWER BACK

The lower back inevitably finds itself in a position of forward bending: a flexion of the spinal column which starts at the neck and travels all the way to the pelvis. This forward flexion brings the vertebrae close together, compromising the discs, which are designed to maintain a cushioned space between each vertebra. This pressure, over time, can create a disc that bulges (commonly referred to as a slipped disc) or ruptures, both of which affect the spinal cord and can cause debilitating pain.

Sitting in this forward flexion stretches and weakens the multifidi (*see* Chapter 2), significantly decreasing their sensitivity to potential movement, and in some cases they can switch off completely. This leaves the vertebrae of the lower back vulnerable to movement, lifting, carrying and other forms of loading. The larger, more superficial muscles of the lower back attempt to take over the responsibility for spinal support, which means they have to sit in a high state of tension to minimize movement. This state is on the brink of spasm and if they have been in this position for a period of time, it will not take a dramatic movement to send them into a painful protective response. This is often how back pain occurs; it appears to come from nowhere, but in reality you are unsuspectingly carrying a ticking time-bomb in your pocket, and are surprised when you touch it gently and your pocket blows apart.

SORE SPOTS?

As a physical therapist I have spent hours working on hundreds of people, all of whom at some point or another are surprised when I find a sore spot they never knew existed. This indicates the level of tissue inflammation and subsequent dysfunction that resides within the body that people can be unaware of. By changing how you move, like sitting on different surfaces (the floor) or going barefoot, you can give your own body a workover by loading different cells with different pressures.

THE PELVIC FLOOR

Discussing issues with the pelvic floor is not something that happens very often. It can still be a topic that creates embarrassment and many people will struggle with problems without discussing it or knowing where to turn for help. It is also an area that has encouraged a lot of varying exercises and protocols for strengthening the muscles in this region, but all too often these do not address the real cause of the issue, which is a whole body problem rather than a localized weakness. The pelvic floor muscles are the base of your core. They attach from your sacrum and up onto your pubic bone.

The pelvic floor muscles are responsible, along with ligaments in the area, for holding your organs in your body, the bladder, uterus or prostate and rectum, and for allowing you to go to the bathroom when you need to. Symptoms of weakness in these muscles include urinary incontinence, trouble with bowel movements, painful urination and a feeling of needing to urinate. Childbirth is often blamed for the demise in the strength and integrity of these muscles; the pressure of

weight-bearing (when unsupported through poor alignment) and the very action of giving birth can leave these muscles stretched and unable to act as a supportive sling to the undercarriage of your body. Having said that, pelvic floor problems can also affect women who have never given birth, and men, and riders are particularly at risk because of the pressures created by the saddle.

It is necessary to discuss the pelvic floor, not only because it is part of the core and an essential part of how your body is designed to function, but also because riding has such a direct impact on the health of this region, for both men and women. Riding places pressure on the muscles of the pelvic floor for which they were never designed. Their role was to be a sling, a responder to downward pressure between two points of alignment: the sacrum and the pubic bone. When the body is moved as it was intended, with the pelvis in a neutral position and the ribs stacked on top of the hips and the hips on top of the heels, the bowl of the pelvis ensured that the tension on this muscle was just right for each individual's personal biological and anatomical make-up. In a body designed to be loaded from above and resisting gravity, the pelvic

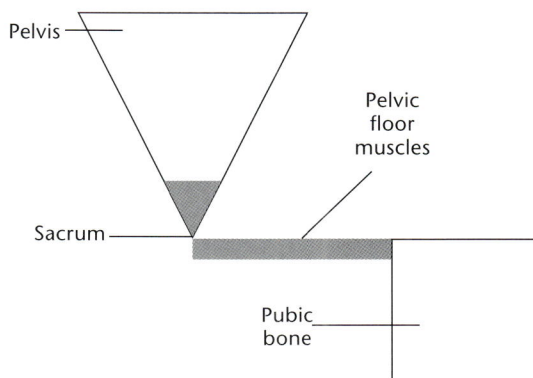

Fig. 23 The correct position of the pelvic floor muscles: the sacrum and pubic bone are aligned and the muscles are of an optimum length.

muscles received enough load to maintain sufficient strength to be an essential member of the core team. In the modern culture of sitting down and sitting on the sacrum (i.e. with the pelvis tucked under) or, for riders, sitting in the saddle, this group of muscles is not subjected to the right amount of load to stay healthy. On top of that, the positioning of the pelvis remains out of neutral as it is not supported through natural movements such as regular squatting, so very little in the way of daily movement is helping to create good tone in the pelvic floor. Sitting in the saddle places upward pressure on these muscles, which they were never designed to deal with. There is nothing to support or cushion this area from pressure from the saddle, so it can become 'bent out of shape', stretched and weakened. Riders also may have a tendency to subconsciously draw the pelvic floor muscles upwards when they are riding as a protective measure and this continuous contraction also renders these muscles useless. In either scenario the pelvic floor can become inflamed and irritated, adding to the pile of poor movement debris that can contribute to pelvic floor disorder.

Tension vs stretch

Pelvic floor disorders can occur either because the muscles are too tight or because they are too stretched and weak, and people with such problems are often advised that their pelvic floor muscles need to be stronger. Exercises and protocols ('see a door, pelvic floor') to encourage a contraction of the muscles has been the advice for decades on how to solve the problem of bladder weakness and the concerning issue of organs heading southward. The problem with working a muscle in isolation is that it doesn't take into consideration how that muscle really works or responds to movement. The muscles of the

pelvic floor attach to the sacrum at the base of the spine and the pubic bone at the front (bottom) of the pelvis. This means the pelvic floor muscles are affected by the relationship (distance) between these two bony landmarks. The sacrum is designed to be able to move (we have seen how it floats against the bones of the pelvis) so that during squatting (intended childbirth and toileting posture) the lower glutes can move the sacrum to increase the space within the pelvis by taking the pressure off the pelvic floor and allowing bathroom and birthing muscles to relax. This release to normal resting length is essential to the health of these muscles and to the healthy functioning of the organs within the pelvis. If you constantly hold the pelvic floor muscles in contraction (which you might be doing without even realizing, especially when riding), you are casting them into a contraction, which creates *tension* but no *tone*. This tension will fight against the activity of your glutes; if your pelvic floor muscles are tighter or gripping more strongly than your glutes then your pelvic floor muscles are actually unusable and the entire holistic functioning of the pelvis is compromised.

The problem with tension

A muscle that is hypertonic is a muscle that cannot do its job. The pelvic floor muscles are made from the same type of skeletal muscle fibres as your biceps or your hamstrings. If you were to isolate these muscles – for example in a bicep curl or hamstring curl at the gym, you lift the weight to contract the muscle and then you lower the arm or leg back to its optimal length before lifting the weight and contracting the muscle again. If you did not do so, and instead just kept holding the bicep or hamstring in a shortened state, you would have permanently bent and unusable limbs. This is what can happen to the pelvic floor

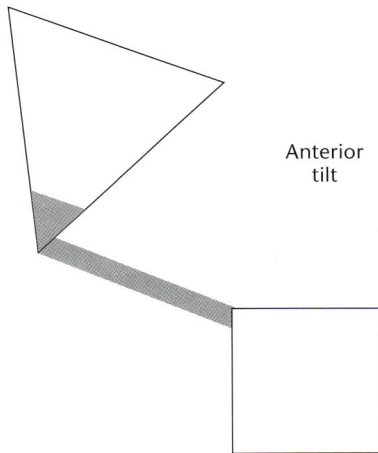

Fig. 24 Pelvic floor muscles – stretched. The sacrum has lifted at the back, a typical result of the pelvis being in anterior rotation, which pulls the muscles of the pelvic floor too tight. This means they are unable to contract and relax, creating disorders of the pelvic floor.

when you actively try to contract the muscles, or your pelvis is in a position that forces it to have too much tension.

If the positioning and tension remain, over time the pelvic floor muscles exert so much force onto the sacrum that they pull it out of alignment, tipping it downwards, which takes the muscle insertion closer to the pubic bone. This shift then takes the tension out of the pelvic floor muscles, leaving them slack and unable to do their job.

The problem with slack

When the pelvic floor muscles have become slack, due to a rotation of the sacrum or due to pressure from the saddle, they can become switched off to sensory/nerve input and will therefore be unable to contract. In this case, small active contractions of the pelvic floor muscles can be useful to reconnect the

dialogue between these muscles and the brain, but the biggest shift is going to come from correct loading via a neutral pelvis and more pelvic movements that support the activation of the glutes. The glutes will help to prevent the sacrum from being pulled out of alignment and when they are able to fire correctly, they provide the right amount of leverage for the pelvic floor muscles to act against. Getting the pelvis into neutral, loading the body in alignment and building a regular squatting practice is the best journey back to pelvic floor health.

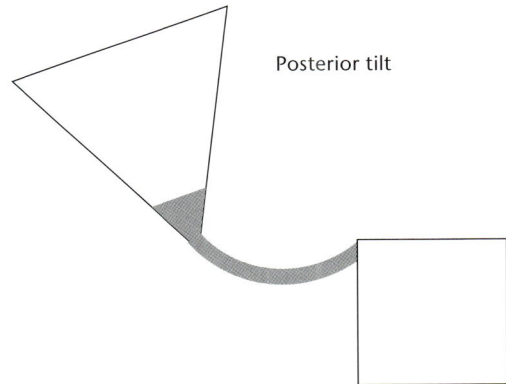

Fig. 25 Pelvic floor muscles – slack. The pelvis has rotated underneath the body, bringing the sacrum closer to the pubic bone. This takes any positive tension out of these muscles, so they are now sitting like a hammock and are unable to provide any support to the undercarriage of the body.

SITTING AND THE UPPER BODY

Gravity is always having an effect on the body, whether you are actively resisting it or not, and it is the upper body that will show the most obvious effects. You know that you only have to give gravity an inch and it will take a mile; place your glass of wine slightly too close to the edge of the table and you will find out how unforgiving it can be. As you sit at your desk for hour after hour during the day, or drive your car, or stand, the chances are your upper body is going to move in front of your hips, however many ergonomic chairs you have and the set-up guidelines you try to adhere to. As soon as your shoulders are in front of your hips they are at the mercy of gravity's downward force. The likelihood is you won't even know it is happening until one day you look in the mirror and wonder why you have rounded shoulders and an exaggerated lump at the base of your neck where you have been sticking your chin forwards and loading the top of your spine and changing the shape and position of your bones.

As gravity exerts its pull on your upper body, the shoulder joints rotate forwards and inwards, shortening the muscles of the front of your chest (the pectorals). The shoulder joints become stuck in a position of forward rotation, which over time impacts how much arm mobility you will have. With a body that has been placed in this position for a long period of time, movements like getting your arms above your head become as foreign to the body as a new language.

Shoulder anatomy

The shoulder joint consists of the head of the humerus (the upper arm bone) and the scapula (shoulder blade). It is a ball and socket joint, and as such is capable of a large amount of movement. The scapula attaches via soft tissues to the vertebrae of the thoracic spine.

If the upper body has been influenced by gravity, the head of the humerus rotates forwards and inwards, pulling the scapula forwards and weakening the connection of the arms to the body. This weakening of the shoulder's positional and attachment muscles means that the shoulder girdle is less able to resist the effects of gravity and the vicious cycle is in full effect. As you saw in Chapter 2, the spine is not a self-supporting structure. The muscles at the back of the body are responsible for counteracting the downward pull of gravity

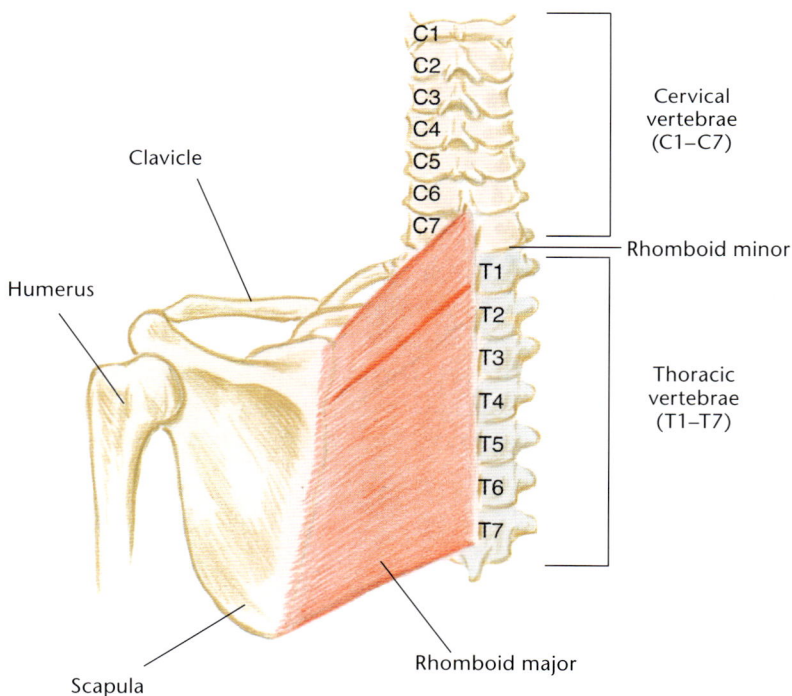

Fig. 26 **The scapula is connected to the body via muscles that attach to the thoracic vertebrae. The strength of the arms is dependent on the strength of this attachment.**

but when the structural framework of the body is out of alignment, these muscles are at the mercy of becoming loaded, stretched and weakened by the downward force gravity exerts. Just as your wine glass topples off the table, so your shoulders will topple off your torso.

From this forward-falling position of the upper body, the chin starts to move forward and away from the neck. The head is a very heavy part of the body, and it should be placed squarely on top of the neck vertebrae so they are not subjected to any loads that may force them out of alignment. Tension in the neck, headaches, inability to look over your shoulder(s) and vertebrae/disc degeneration are some of the symptoms you might experience as a result of this posture.

The shoulder girdle

The scapula, thoracic vertebrae and shoulder joint make up the shoulder girdle. It is a trio of parts that come together as a whole, each influencing the function of the other. The strength of the arms is dependent upon the strength of their attachment to the body, which is dependent on the health of the muscles that attach the scapula to the spine. Your arms can carry load and they can lift weight but they are only as strong as their attachment to the body. Think of branches of a tree; if their attachment to the trunk is secure, they can withstand high winds, leaves loaded with rain and even people swinging from them. If, however, their attachment is compromised, these events will challenge how well the branch can stay connected to the trunk.

Arms, like tree branches, are not part of the structural column of the human body so they are rarely associated with posture, but they do have a postural function; poor arm positioning exerts a drag on the neck, the ribs and the way the body can breathe. Structural misalignments through shoulder position, and the relationship of the trunk and shoulder girdle, will all affect how the arms are able to function.

Your body was designed to have arms strong enough both to push objects away from the body and to bring the body towards the hands, and this strength was garnered through constant use for small, low-grade loading and movements such as preparing food, as well as larger, more complex loads such as carrying water and firewood. These constant loads kept the muscles that attach the scapula to the spine nice and strong as well as keeping the vertebrae of the upper body in an upright position. Movement habits that require little movement or strength from the arms (such as typing at a computer) weaken the connection and interaction of the components of the shoulder girdle. Weaknesses in this region can have a significant impact on how you ride as the level of strength of your shoulder girdle is directly related to the quality of the contact you will be able to provide your horse.

Your arms are intended to be able to lift above your head, reach in front of you, reach behind you and out to the sides. When the upper arm gets stuck and the head of your humerus starts folding inwards in the socket, these natural, fundamental movements begin to be removed from your repertoire. Maybe you struggle to get your arms above your head and you have adjusted how you get dressed, or you have suffered with a 'frozen shoulder' or pain between your shoulder-blades. Maybe you do not even realize that your arms are not as mobile as they should be – at least until you have a tall horse to tack up, requiring you to lift your arms above you to get the saddle on. If your shoulders are stuck, the reach has to come from somewhere else in your body. Typically you will thrust your ribs and hyperextend your lower back, which creates microtrauma in your lower back every time you do it.

When your shoulders are restricted, simple movements like putting the saddle on can cause you to hyperextend your back and thrust your ribs.

It's all an illusion

When the upper body begins to curl forward, the shape you are seeing on the outside is the result of the vertebrae folding forwards. This curvature is accompanied by the scapula moving forward and away from the spine, weakening the connection of the arms to the body. As this curve becomes more obvious, people try to correct their posture by pulling their shoulders back. It is a postural correction for riders that is heard all over the world: 'shoulders back, sit up straight!' Some people are taught to bring their scapulae

together and downwards, and before I knew more, that is the correction I too would give riders, because aesthetically this appeared to do the job. The chest would be open, the arms would be stabilized by anchoring the scapulae and the arms could stay elastic in the saddle. The problem was that the scapulae had only been moved relative to the ground and not to the spine, so instead of creating a strengthening, aligned posture, this correction only served to cast the muscles between the scapulae and the still folded-forward vertebrae into contraction. This tension is inhibitory not just for the quality of contact when riding (*see* Chapter 4), but also for the rider's body to function in the saddle with any level of coordination or synchronization with the horse. The stretched and weak muscles between the scapulae and the spine are now asked to contract and to maintain that contraction for a prolonged period of time, which is a position they are not strong enough to hold. The forward bending/positioning of the vertebrae is still very much there, which means the true functioning quality of the shoulder girdle has not been improved; it has just had more tension added onto it. As a rider you will become sore trying to hold this correction, and you will not be able to replicate it for long when riding on your own without a cue from your instructor because it is an inhibitory move rather than a strengthening correction. To really strengthen this area and to change the position of the vertebrae, corrective movements have to be done on the ground.

RIB-CAGE, LUNGS AND BREATHING

In Chapter 2 you saw how your body was designed to function. Part of its mechanical make-up is having a long, strong, open torso. This is to ensure that the rib-cage (and therefore the lungs housed within the ribs) has ample room to fully expand. Only from this fully expanded position is the thoracic spine properly supported, and the limbs able to move independently from the trunk. Sitting and collapsing the upper body forwards prevents the ribs from lifting up and out, which means the diaphragm does not work with any strength. Breathing becomes very shallow, the body does not relax, the amount of oxygen delivery is reduced and it means that the entire mid-section of the body is never fully supported. This may not be an obvious problem whilst sitting and having little or no demands placed on the body, but as soon as you start moving and you carry the effects of this seated posture into standing and riding, the weakness, co-dependence and poor respiratory health become significant performance inhibitors, whether you are aware of it or not.

Using the entire rib-cage to breathe (including the intercostals and the diaphragm) means that the front of the core receives load and activation, helping to strengthen the whole area. If you consider you will take between 23,000 and 25,000 breaths every day, it becomes a fantastic opportunity to improve the health of your body without having to make extra time or pay a gym membership to do it. In Chapter 6 you will be taken through the mechanics of breathing and how it can affect your riding.

HYPERTONICITY

Hypertonicity describes the state of a muscle when it habitually sits in a position of tension that is more than it was designed to cope with, for longer than it should. Hypertonicity can affect the muscle at a cellular level (*see* Chapter 1).

GET TO THE CAUSE

Your body might well be a powerful machine, but just like a car with faulty steering, it's probably a mistake to try to accelerate out of trouble or to put cleaner fuel in it to try to fix the problem. A mechanical problem requires a mechanical fix, and it's the same for your body. There is no need to wait for the inevitable accident to put the tools you have to better use.

SITTING DOWN 'EXTRAS'

Maybe you don't just sit down. Maybe you add a little something extra, like crossing your legs. Movement habits creep into every area, and the way you sit is no exception. The likelihood that you cross your legs without thinking about it and cross them the same way each time is very high, and this consistent loading pattern creates a predictable reaction in the body.

Let's suppose you take your right leg over your left. This will stretch the right glute, contract and activate the right hip flexor and adductor, and bring the hip joint forward and into internal rotation. In order to prevent the entire upper body from tipping to the right (as you have removed the loading ability of the right side of the pelvis), the muscles on the left side of the lower back have to shorten and contract to hold you upright.

Sitting in this posture creates an ideal environment for rotation through the pelvis, causing different tensions in each side of the back and around the hips: a true postural sling imbalance in action. This variance in tension creates a pelvis that is asymmetric, which means it will interact with movement loads differently on each side from both your own loading and the loads you will experience from your horse. Riding is a sport that relies upon, demands and can only be successful from a place of symmetry (or at the very least from a place where the impact of asymmetry is minimized). The body you bring to the saddle determines how successful at this you are going to be, and one that has been creating a pelvic twist for eight hours a day whilst seated with crossed legs is going to have muscles in different states of tension, which means the position of the pelvis is going to be crooked. This will affect how the horse can use his hindquarters but it will also affect how your body is able to cope with the loads it has to deal with from your horse. Muscles in tension are not able to absorb and subsequently transfer the loads they experience, so everything that comes from the horse into your body on the side of tension in the pelvis is hit with resistance. To deal with it the body has to find some way to cope and this is when you get an exaggerated head nod in the sitting trot, or a bouncing in the saddle in canter or a leg gripping up. Some postural adjustment will be made to try to compensate for the forces coming into the body that are not being absorbed at the point of entry: the pelvis.

Asymmetry through the pelvis

Having a pelvis that rotates one way and sits with one hip in front of the other is a common postural problem that many people have, and more than most riders have. This is due to a difference in the loads that each side of the pelvis, spine and shoulders have received when moving and when sitting, which creates more of a pull towards one side than the other. This position means that one hip is sitting slightly ahead of the other in the saddle, creating a difference in weight distribution through the seat bones, which means the horse will move his hindquarters differently to match what is happening. This situation is two-fold, as a

horse who is moving crookedly will also impact how the pelvis of the rider has to absorb load. A horse who does not move straight, or pushes unevenly with his hind legs, will exert a different amount of force through each side of his pelvis. His rider's pelvis will therefore receive different loads every time he is ridden. This asymmetric loading over time can influence the state of the tissues of the lumbar spine and groin and those surrounding the hip, which can pull both your and your horse's pelvis even further out of alignment.

STANDING UP

It may not seem as though sitting down has created any negative patterns to your body, as you believe you are able to get into an upright position just by standing up. Well, sadly the biomechanics of your body beg to differ. After sitting down for a period of time your body maintains the adaptations of the chair within the tissues. This means that you carry with you the length, tone and skeletal positioning as if you were still sitting down, so in order to appear upright, your body has to go through some significant postural adaptations.

NEUTRAL PELVIS, RIBS AND SPINE

Neutral pelvis

As described in Chapter 2, the pelvis is a three-dimensional bowl and in order to be in 'neutral' (where the tail bone is neither tucked underneath nor lifted up at the back) there are parameters that it needs to sit within. The pelvis can be in three different positions: neutral, in an anterior tilt or in a posterior tilt.

If you spend time in a seated position, the muscles that influence the position of the pelvis all have to deal with different loads, because of the geometry of the bones. Recalling the guy rope analogy on the tent in Chapter 2, the muscles that control the position of the pelvis are forced into different tensions that do not unravel when you stand up.

Sitting, as you have seen, requires the hips to come into a ninety-degree angle of flexion. This means the hip flexors (the muscles that attach to the thigh and the pelvis) are required to shorten as the bones come closer together.

It is very common for a lot of people to sit with the tailbone tucked underneath them, which means the sacrum is being loaded. The pelvic bowl is tipping down at the back, the lumbar spine is flexing (curving the wrong way) and the muscles at the front are being increasingly shortened as the space between the pelvis and the thigh is reduced. This is known as a posterior pelvic tilt.

From this position you can see that the hips will not be able to get into full extension, and the upper body is going to be affected by the draw of gravity as the shoulders move in front of the hips.

When you come to stand up, the tight muscles that want to pull your hips towards your nose do not unravel. They maintain their contracted state, which means mechanically you are still bent in half and the thighs are in front of the pelvis. When you stand up and the hips need to become more vertical, the hip flexors can pull the front of the pelvis down towards the ground in what is known as an anterior pelvic tilt. This posture means that the pelvic bowl would now pour water out of the front. The tail bone is lifted and the weight of the body is pushed over the knees.

The hip flexors and the psoas muscle will be affecting how the pelvis sits. Tight hip flexors will pull the top of the pelvis downwards and a tight psoas will bring the lumbar spine into flexion, which encourages the pelvis to sit in a tucked position. Both of these postures take the pelvis out of neutral, as well as altering the position of the hips and the shape of the

Sitting down often causes a tucking-under of the pelvis, with the loads taken on the sacrum rather than the seat bones, affecting the position of the pelvis when you stand up.

YOUR BODY TELLS A STORY

Your standing posture will tell the story of how your body is masking tension in areas that cannot move. Rib thrust is one clue, pelvic tilt is another, over-pronation of the feet is another. Whenever you move the body in a way that is not aligned, your body is compensating for tension and it is this tension that will lead to dysfunction, pain, injury and a wearing-out of structures.

lower back, and both of these positions impact how you sit in the saddle and therefore how your horse is able to move. This is discussed in further detail in Chapter 4.

RIB THRUST

When you move to a standing posture, the body wants to be upright and it wants to keep the eyes level. As you have seen, actually standing upright and appearing to stand upright can be two very different things, and if your body is adjusting from being chair-shaped it has to find compensatory mechanisms to counteract this imbalance of a lower body that is trying to keep itself folded in half; segments of your body that *can* move find a way to move around other segments that cannot. The next available area to manoeuvre when the pelvis and hips cannot is the thoracic spine and rib-cage, so it is at this level that further imbalances come into play. When you sit down, the front of the body is shortened and when you stand up, this needs to be lengthened in order to get your upper body to

be upright. However, when the hips and pelvis are being pulled downwards and the angle of the thigh relative to the pelvis has been reduced, the ability to extend the front of the body is challenging. In order to get the chest upright, the ribs are thrust forwards and out beyond the level of your pelvis. This movement does not cause a flexion or extension of the spine, but rather a 'shearing' of the vertebrae, creating a step effect, and the appearance of an increased lumbar curve.

Not only does this posture push the upper body forwards and away from the load-bearing hips, it also tenses and compresses the lower spine. This makes the lower back vulnerable to movement, lifting and carrying, as well as reducing its ability to absorb movement from the horse. The upper body is also compromised as the shoulders and neck experience a dragging tensile load from the ribs being pulled forwards, which creates stiffness and weakness of the entire shoulder girdle area that extends into the neck.

The thoracic area of the spine is the region that is designed for the most rotation, and when the vertebrae are stacking on top

POSITION OF VERTEBRAE DURING RIB THRUST

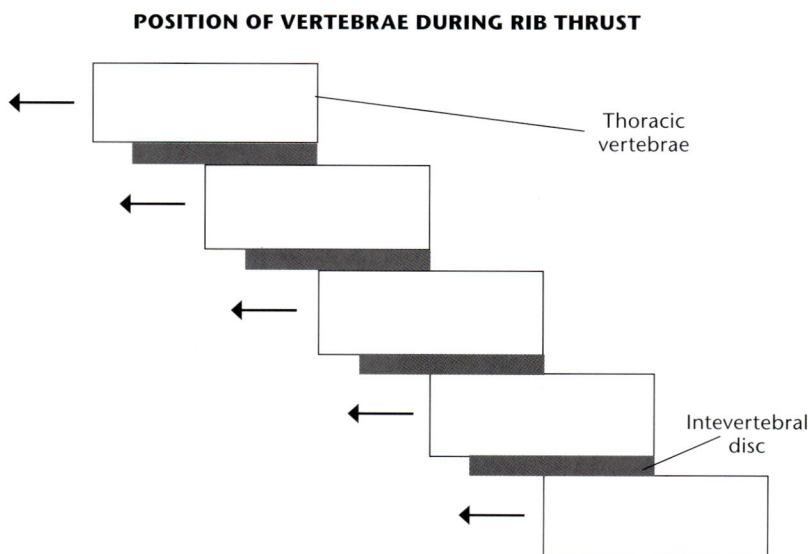

Thoracic vertebrae

Intevertebral disc

Fig. 27 When the ribs are pushed upwards and forwards, the vertebrae are forced into a shearing or forward stepping position, which leaves the joints and discs vulnerable to movement and load.

of each other, this rotation is possible. If the ribs move into a stepped or a shearing position, any twisting movement can be really damaging and problems can occur when exercises at the gym or in a class fail to address the rib thrust first. To make any exercise safe for the spine, the ribs must first be dropped back down to where they should be, sitting above the pelvis. If you add a twist to a thrusted rib-cage it is similar to applying the same torque to your discs as wringing out a wet dishcloth. This is why twisting movements with load can be so damaging to your back, and why it is generally considered a movement to be avoided.

WAIST MOBILITY

The muscles of the waist are designed for stabilizing the spine and for allowing movement of the mid-section of the body. If this area of the body was not designed to move, the ribs would extend all the way to the pelvis. This would mean that the internal organs would be protected, but it would remove the body's ability to bend and twist, which were crucial movements for foraging in varying environments. The mobility of the waist is essential to building strength in the core and this mobility of the mid-section allows the upper body and the pelvis to move independently from each other; a crucial ability for riding in balance. Having a waist that can move above the pelvis in the saddle is critical for riders who want to absorb their horse's movement and appear to sit 'still'.

THE MOVEMENT HABIT

Humans are creatures of habit, which means that much of what you do each day comes from a place of autopilot. Some of this can be really useful but the brain cannot distinguish a good habit from a bad one, so left unchecked, habits have the potential to be damaging to your health. The brain's ability to form habits has enabled innovation, creation and problem solving on an incredible scale. Habit formation gives the brain space to think intellectually so that it can advance the potential survival of the species. Having a system that creates habits means that mundane, everyday tasks are relegated to the caretaker of habit and therefore do not

WATCH YOUR FORM

It is common in many classes when doing any movements lying on your back to be told to press your lower back into the floor as this 'engages the core' and helps to strengthen it, whilst 'protecting the lumbar spine'. One of the reasons this has been necessary is because of rib thrust and adding movements on top of a thrusted rib-cage can be damaging to the spine. The more beneficial way to reap a reward from exercises done lying on your back would be to bolster the rib-cage and shoulders so that the body is aligned. This removes the shearing position of the vertebrae, making the body aligned and ready to cope with movement from the waist and limbs. This is a much more functional position for the body because when you actively press your lower back into the floor, you are casting the muscles of your waist into a contraction, which means they cannot gain any strength from the movement you are about to do. Bolster the ribs and allow your waist (and therefore the muscles of the core) to move and strengthen according to the exercise you are doing.

require complex brain activity. Habits do not just apply to the things you 'do', they also apply to how you move and use your body. Just as the brain does not want to think about how to get dressed, it also doesn't want to think about how you walk or stand or drive or sit. Movement awareness is removed as the brain uses its energy for new, potentially life-threatening activities or more complex, analytical thinking. By relegating movement to habit, you stop taking notice of what your body is doing, and which parts are working and which parts are not, and this applies both on and off the horse.

You have been developing movement habits ever since you started to move. As a child you would have explored how your body could move in the world, and you also would have picked up movement habits from one or both of your parents; just as you learnt speech, you also copied postures from the people around you. Maybe your left foot turns out, just like your mum's, or maybe you stand with your weight over one leg, like your dad. It is not uncommon for postural habits to take hold at an early age, and in the case of the turning-out foot, it might be that your mum had arthritis in that hip, and now you seem to be heading down the same road. Hereditary? Unavoidable? Probably not; it is more likely just a movement habit that you adopted, placing the same loads on the hip as your mum did; maybe her mum did the same.

If you aren't sure what movement habits you have created, try answering these questions:

1. How do you stand when you are talking to someone? Where is your weight distributed? Which direction are your feet pointing?
2. How do you stand when you brush your teeth?
3. What shape do you put your lower back into when you put the saddle on?
4. Which shoe do you put on first?
5. Which arm do you reach to grab things with?
6. What else were you thinking about when you reversed the car out of the driveway this morning?

Chances are you had to pause to answer some or all of these questions, even though they are probably movements and activities that you do every day. The power of habit is incredibly useful; it means you can think about other things whilst washing up, making a drink, grooming the horse or mucking out. However, the downside of habit as it relates to movement is that the ability to be body aware becomes diluted. Repetitive actions reduce the activity of the brain so it will stop taking notice, or alerting you to the position your body is in. For most people, most of the time, this isn't a life-threatening issue; it doesn't necessarily serve the mechanic of the body in the best way, and will certainly play a major role in how the body looks, functions and feels, but not being aware of how you stand when you brush your teeth is unlikely to lead to a meeting with your maker.

Riding, however, relies on the rider to be incredibly body aware; to know where it is in time and space, to know how each part is positioned and how this is affecting every other part, and how that positioning is potentially affecting the horse. Poor positional habits in the saddle are carried over from poor movement habits on the ground. If you have ever had your position corrected only for it to feel wrong, crooked or weird, it is because your brain is desperately trying to reconcile the new information. It begins a battle of wanting to keep the energy-saving habit but is unable to ignore the new behaviour, as it might be an issue of survival. You have, in essence, woken the sleeping giant who wants to make a new sequence of movement feel out of the ordinary so it can just go back to sleep again.

The repetitive nature of riding and training means that you will organize the body in the saddle in a way that feels normal, comfortable and 'correct'. You will ride your horse with the same technique from a body in the same position every time you get on. If you always ride by kicking, fiddling, leaning or gripping, your brain will not recognize that these are happening because it will relegate them to the 'habit' category. If you take lessons, your instructor may tell you to keep your legs still or to keep your left arm down and for a few minutes your attention will be focused on the 'fix' you have been given. You will possibly be able to maintain this new awareness whilst your instructor provides the reminder but it is likely to be diverted once you are asked to do something new or more complex. Your brain will immediately kick into action for acquiring information on the new task, which sends the old kicking or arm waving habit right back into the deep dark depths of the container of habit. It is important to know that in times of stress or vulnerability, you will always default to the level of your strongest habit.

Body awareness is key to both a better functioning body and also the ability to improve your position in the saddle. Habits that are already formed can neither be improved nor destroyed, but through persistent tiny drips every day, they can be changed if you know what they are.

THE HABIT LOOP

Habits rely on the brain to stop taking notice of actions and behaviours that frequently occur. Awareness, diligence and corrections require a constant level of energy that could be detrimental to survival and as we are still operating from an ancient emotional brain, it cannot afford to be consumed with the minutiae of life. According to Charles Duhigg (*The Power of Habit*), the process of converting a sequence of actions into an automatic routine is known as 'chunking'. We rely on dozens (maybe hundreds) of behavioural 'chunks' every day.

In order to create a sequence, there are three components that must be present:

Trigger: this tells the brain to go on automatic pilot and which habit to use;
Routine: this is the action; physical, mental or emotional; and
Reward: this helps the brain determine if the loop is worth remembering.

The basal ganglia

The basal ganglia is the habit epicentre of the brain. It is about the size of a golfball and is able to store your habits, in their entirety, for the duration of your life. If this area is undamaged (through disease or trauma), people who have suffered an injury to another part of the brain and who may not remember their own age, are still able to cook, find their way home and tie shoelaces. The neurological sequencing of their habits is stored and the person can still carry out complex behaviours. Understanding this is incredibly useful if you want to make actual changes to the way you move your body.

The habit loop of trigger, routine, reward is a powerful sequence for the brain because after a while of repeating this loop, an emotional response of anticipation and craving is stimulated. The saying that old habits die hard is totally correct; in fact, old habits don't die at all; however, whilst habits cannot be improved or destroyed, the routine or behaviour section can be replaced. Once you know the trigger, you can implement a new behaviour that will reap the original reward until a new habit is born.

So how does this relate to the way you move?

The biggest requirement to improving the function and appearance of your body (from a biomechanical perspective) starts with being aware of what the body naturally wants to do. This means to notice the movement habit loops the brain has created through your patterns of repetitive movements.

The way you walk, how long it takes you to cross your legs when you sit down, the way you lean over your computer, the way you tack up your horse, the way you muck out, the way you pick out feet, the way you carry water buckets, the way you sit in the car will all have habit loops, which means you do not have to think about the actual process of doing any of them. You will be able to hold a conversation, think about what to cook for dinner or the email you need to send whilst driving, tacking up, mucking out and cleaning your teeth. This is your basal ganglia at work. People who have been riding for a while will have movement habits in the saddle too. The way you hold your head, rest your feet in the stirrups, move your arms or hands up or down, how you collapse one side of your body, or the way you kick every stride or fiddle with the contact.

So how do you insert a new behaviour/ habit? As with most behaviours that you would like to change, the first step is always awareness – in particular awareness of how you are moving and what you are doing with your body. In terms of your riding posture, you could get a friend to video you. If you have seen yourself on camera and been shocked by some of your positional traits, this is the first step to awareness, but also you will now understand that this is the habit cycle in action. It is perfectly natural for you not to notice everything you do in the saddle. Remember, your body is an excellent adaptor and it is quite prepared to make you do strange things in the saddle if it means avoiding using the weak bit,

the tight bit, or the bit that has fallen asleep. And because you are not aware of which those bits are, your brain tends to focus on the main job at hand: getting the horse going. In that quest, the attention to where your body is in time and space and relative to the horse is forgotten. As you have just seen, your brain will tell you that the head tilt is normal, or that collapsing one way feels straight because you have made it a habit to sit like that. By seeing the position your body is habitually programmed to be in, you can start to change the way it behaves. This knowledge should be very empowering; by knowing what you are doing and having the tools to correct it (see the following chapters), you are able to change how your body operates both on and off the horse.

When we start to realize how disconnected from our bodies we have become on the ground, it is not hard to understand why we do not realize what we are doing on the horse. The key is to change our habits on the ground and become more body aware so that we develop movement 'cues' that trigger us in the saddle.

A SIMPLE START

Making a positive change to habit behaviour does not have to start with a huge gesture. Small, seemingly trivial behavioural changes can set the stage for more significant habits you would like to adjust. Take a look at something as simple as brushing your teeth. The trigger for the habit is the time of day and you standing at the sink. As you pick up your toothbrush the habit loop is activated. The action is of course the actual brushing and the reward is a clean fresh set of teeth. Without thinking about it, you will use your dominant hand every time. You probably won't want to change the habit of cleaning your teeth, but you might want to challenge the brain by doing the brushing with your non-dominant hand. You know the habit loop is secure so all you need to do is be aware and pass the toothbrush to the other hand. If you repeat this with awareness, it can become a new habit. Teaching the mind that this is possible through 'small wins' starts a mindset that can be incredibly useful when you want to adjust something bigger. When it comes to riding performance, lessons can be learnt from mindset and habit creation from top performing athletes. Many rely on a routine, which is just a series of habits that are done every time before a competition, in the same way. The key is to make the formation of these habits intentional, so that you know they are serving you and your performance in a positive way.

THE PAIN EPIDEMIC

Living with pain is not a natural state to be in. It may have become 'normal' for society collectively, but it is certainly not the destination of choice or intent of the body. Your body has a blueprint for health, comfort, function, strength and durability and it strives to fulfil these areas constantly. It works incredibly hard to keep functioning as well as it can, but it is constrained by the food you provide it and the movement you ask of it. Humans are not designed to be in physical pain for a prolonged period of time as it is so detrimental to survival but as a master adaptor, it will bend, sculpt, stretch and contract in response to everything you do – but it does not have an endless capacity for altering its state. At some point it will reach its limit and this is when you will start to experience stiffness, muscle spasm, aches and then pain. Pain is an indicator that damage has occurred and that the tissues require different input if catastrophic breakdown is to be avoided. For many of us, life was probably relatively pain-

free up to a certain point and then aches and pains started to creep in, often attributed to the unavoidable timeline of ageing. However, what is abundantly clear is that your movement environment, your movement habits and your body awareness are the triad that can create your pain or steer you away from it. Riders show up in the saddle in pain all too often. In fact, the majority of riders that I work with have varying levels of pain to deal with, from the insidious grumbling hip to chronic, movement-inhibiting sciatica; pain seems to be an ever-present companion and it is impacting riders on a number of levels. Mental health, physical well-being and riding performance are all compromised if you are in pain. The added dimension for riders is that the pain they bring to the saddle will also affect the way their horse can move. Pain in your body is not benign; even if you have reached for every pain-inhibiting protocol available to you – medication, tape, heat and ice – the damage is still present. As a response to tissue pain, the body starts to protect the damaged site and therefore compromises how other tissues work so that the affected area is not overloaded. This means that the movement, sensory input and response of the entire body are all affected and this effect will be felt by the horse. For example, riding with a sore back will give your horse a sore back, and he will change how he moves within six weeks.

THE LOWER BACK FIASCO

The World Health Organization cites lower back pain as the leading cause of disability in the world, while in the UK the NHS states that more days off work are due to crippling lower back pain than any other 'illness'. The World Back Care Organization claims that it affects more people than breast cancer, diabetes and heart disease combined. If you have ever suffered with lower back pain you will know all too well how impactful on your life it can be. It can greet you as soon as you get out of bed, or try to stand upright after picking out your horse's feet. The interesting aspect of back pain is that everyone seems vulnerable to it, from elite athletes to the cliché couch potato. No single body seems to be immune to the spontaneous back spasm or debilitating consistent pain. Is it really a fault in the system? Or is the system not being used correctly? Is the body really that susceptible to lower back trouble? To unravel the explanation behind lower back pain, we take into account the information we have covered so far: repetitive movement habits and the effects of sitting. But does this explain enough? These topics may cast some light on why a sedentary person may experience back pain, but it does not complete the story, given that elite athletes from professional tennis players to Tour de France cyclists experience the same problem. Why are these issues present in the sporting elite, in athletes who should be in a highly functioning body that is being moved a lot of the day?

The practice of focusing on the 'six-pack' (the front of the body and abdominal muscle group) has created an obsession that has dominated the fitness industry for the past two decades. The message has been that a sore lower back is the fault of a weak core, and the part that needs to be strengthened to 'protect' the lower back is the front of the torso. It has also become a cultural phenomenon that contoured abdominals are the most aesthetically pleasing. Drawing the tummy button towards the spine and doing more sit-ups has been an unchallenged prescription for the global failure of the lower back. For equestrian sport, rider fitness has had to take its directives from the mainstream fitness industry and as a result, most protocols centre around the same message. Riders are a group of athletes who seem particularly vulnerable to lower back pain. The seated position (angle of

hips), saddle design and fit, movement loads and forces from the horse all impact the lower back of the rider. It stands to reason that a lower back that has already been weakened through poor movement and posture will not cope with the forces, and will lack the adaptability required of tissues necessary to maintain the health of the back when riding. The *effect* of this impact is determined by the state of health of the lower back before even sitting in the saddle, rather than riding being the main cause of back pain. Riding can aggravate a lower back that is already not functioning well off the horse. Considering how the core should operate (being led by the lower back musculature) and considering how modern movement habits weaken and switch off the vertebral support, it is not surprising that trying to absorb the horse's movement, hold the rider in position, affect the movement of the horse, and stay in balance and synchronicity is a step too far for a back that is not supported by muscular health. This can lead to disc problems, vertebral degeneration, muscular spasm and nerve pain. When these issues present themselves in riders, it is easy to point to riding as the cause, when in reality the cause lies in the way the body has been used and moved out of the saddle, and riding is simply the catalyst to damage.

Unfortunately, when the lower back musculature is weak and abused through poor movement, it cannot stabilize the spine and therefore cannot direct the rest of the core muscles into their roles. Targeting the front of the body (standard 'core' training) without looking after the posterior muscles is similar to communicating vital statistics on a phone with poor signal. Information is lost and the result is unsatisfactory. Without the leadership of the lower back, targeting the front part of the core becomes purely an exercise in shortening the abdominals whilst closing the gap between the vertebrae of the lumbar spine, which ultimately means damage and pain.

The message here is that the lower back needs to be at the top of the list of priorities. When we are able to align and strengthen this area, the abdominals at the front and sides of the body are given a better chance to be able to switch on and carry out their supportive roles with the appropriate level of strength.

Artificial back supports: a note

There are a number of back support devices available to riders, and for some they can be a very appealing solution to chronic and debilitating back pain when riding, or when doing chores. The problem with devices that provide artificial support is that they switch off the body's reflex and internal proprioceptive mechanism which general movement and musculo-skeletal health rely upon. Back braces and supports cast the muscles and vertebrae into a static position, and movement is controlled which therefore reduces pain; whilst the body may feel better when one is worn, what is actually happening is that the muscles are switching off and cell death is occurring. To this end, back braces serve only to weaken an already weak structure and pain should be a guide, a hint, a clue, rather than something to hide. By acknowledging pain, you can accept that there is a problem, and once you know there is a problem, you can work out the solution. In this case, back-strengthening exercises, aligned and frequent movement and postures that strengthen the entire core will lead your body to a place of sustainable comfort rather than give it a temporary hide-out. Of course, if this is the only way you are going to get through the day, practicalities must prevail. The word of caution is that these devices are not a long-term solution.

Author's note: this only applies if you have no diagnosis of vertebral trauma that requires stabilizing!

THE FRONT OF THE TORSO: DIASTASIS RECTI

In Chapter 2 you learnt about the muscles of the front and sides of the torso and how important their health is to the functioning of the entire core. Diastasis recti may not be a term you have heard, or it might be something you know you are dealing with. In a nutshell, diastasis recti is the *unnatural* distance of the rectus abdominus muscles (right and left sides) from the midline of the body. There isn't a standard distance they should be; it will be unique to you, but in the case of diastasis recti, this distance has become abnormal *for you*. It is commonly diagnosed as an issue of pregnancy, when pressures within the body from the growing baby place excess load and tension on the muscles at the front of the torso causing them to move away from the midline. As many riders want to have families and get back in the saddle as quickly as possible after giving birth, it is a worthwhile topic to discuss here. In addition, it is a condition that can affect men just as much as it can pregnant women, so it comes under a whole-body movement issue and is therefore applicable to everyone.

The rectus abdominus muscles are commonly known as your 'six-pack'. They are naturally divided into right and left sides and housed within their own fascia. Chapter 2 outlined the anatomy of the front of the torso, but to recap, all of the abdominal muscles attach via a mesh of tendon-like structures to the linea alba which runs down the centre of the body. Any loads that are placed on the body, either from within (visceral fat, pregnancy, poor breathing patterns, tummy button sucking in, rib thrust or pelvic thrust) or from outside (arm, leg and torso movement), create a tug on this mesh which affects the tension in all the muscles of the 'core'. When the tension is greater on one side of the body than the other, one side of the rectus abdominus can be pulled away from the midline. Likewise, if you have moved with your ribs thrusted or your pelvis pushed forwards, both sides of your rectus abdominus can be pulled into an unnatural distance from the midline. Increasing their distance from the anchor point of the linea alba weakens their ability to contract, which therefore reduces their strength. The ability of the muscles of the front and sides of the torso to contract with strength is key to whole core function and therefore to whole body movement and function. This central part of the body, although guided and led by the lower back, is designed for strong movement patterns in all directions. This is only possible if these muscles are strong and sit at a normal (for you) distance from their anchor point. Riding requires that the core is able to operate from its natural place of responding via reflex to the loads that it experiences. Riding throws massive amounts of load through the core, to which it needs to respond rapidly – in other words, through a reflex. You cannot possibly hope to consciously direct the core to switch on with every step the horse takes: you would stop breathing before you managed five strides. A strong, mobile, connected core is key to mastering the ability to sit in the saddle and adjust your position to stay in synchronicity with the horse. If the muscles at the front of your core are disconnected through too much tension, they will be unable to turn an instruction into an action.

The way you stand, walk, sit, move and breathe, and how much weight you carry around your midline, will all contribute to the possibility of having a diastasis recti. If you are very one-sided, or have an asymmetrical activity that you do a lot of the time, this too can affect the state of the muscles at the front of your body. If you are pregnant or have given birth (particularly more than once), it is extremely likely that your abdominal muscles have migrated from their normal position. The good news is that Part Two includes whole body movements that will help bring these muscles back to where they belong.

What do sit-ups actually do?

One of the problems with a seated posture is that it puts the lower back into a position of flexion, which means a forward-bending posture. This position lengthens and weakens all the musculature of the lower back, from the deep stabilizers to the larger, more superficial muscles (the ones you can touch). It also forces the vertebrae to press/compress the protective, fluid-filled discs between them that provide protection against concussion, vibration and general movement to prevent the vertebrae rubbing against each other and causing the bones to wear away. A position that forces the body to damage these discs is not one it would naturally choose as it makes it very vulnerable to injury and pain. Any action – be it throughout the day or in a fitness class or at the gym – that puts the back into this flexion exacerbates the problems associated with sitting. The action of sit-ups, mountain climbers or any other exercise that brings the spine into flexion, has one objective, and that is to shorten the front of the body. By shortening the front of the torso, you have to lengthen and weaken the back. Whilst it may appear that you are strengthening your 'core', what you are actually doing is taking the lower back further and further away from a place of strength, function and comfort. Flexing the lumbar spine is a catalyst for weakness, damage and therefore pain in this area. As you learnt from the core section, the multifidi which connect the lumbar vertebrae are highly sensitive to movement potential. This means that when the limbs move, suggesting that the body is on the move, these muscles are meant to switch on and stabilize the vertebrae. Flexing the spine stretches these muscles, meaning that they cannot determine or react quickly to the messages they should be receiving. If you liken their communication to an old-fashioned tin can and string 'telephone', you will remember that in order for you to communicate with someone holding the other tin can, the string had to be taut. A slack string does not allow communication to travel without interference, and the message might even be lost on the way. It ends up as a Chinese whispers scenario, which at best results in an unclear message and at worst (when applying it to the body) creates damage. To remedy the problem, the focus needs to move from the front of the body to the back. Strengthening the back secures communication, maintains vertebral positioning (thereby reducing compression of discs) and instructs the other muscles of the core to switch on at the right level for the activity being performed. It is time to change the message that the front of the body is responsible for helping the back. The size of the muscles in each region should be enough to point us all in the right direction. The abdominals are small compared to those at the back; the back is designed to be strong, the front is designed to follow instructions. It is rare to have an employee miss a day of work because of an 'ab strain', but 'throwing your back out' can put you out of work and stop you riding time and time again.

THE AGEING MYTH

Riding as a sport is fairly unusual in that riders of all ages are able to enjoy, compete and train. Most riders, when asked, want to ride 'for as long as their body will let them'. Ageing brings with it an idea that has been cemented into our collective psyche that the failure of the body is an inevitable destination: that you will be unable to move, crippled with pain, and

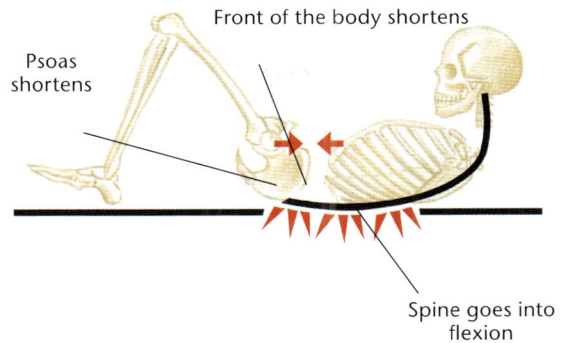

Fig. 28 The standard sit-up focuses on shortening the front of the body, which stretches and weakens the muscles of the lower back as it is moved into flexion. All too often this action also activates the hip flexors, making them shorter and tighter and pulling the pelvis out of alignment.

will have more artificial joints than real ones. Society reinforces this all the time, especially when you see an older person struggling to get out of a car or shuffling along behind a walking frame. The older people in our lives may also support this idea with grumblings over how the body is falling apart, with cries of 'It's my age!' It is true that tissue health declines with age; the cellular make-up of soft tissues changes, making them less elastic, and cell regeneration does stop. Bone density can alter too, but a lot of this is down to nutrition and movement. We certainly do not live in the same body for seventy-five years – organs grow, reduce, improve and decline – but there is no need to surrender to age, blaming it for the aches and pains you experience. Is it your age or is it how you have moved your body?

Society as a whole blames age for the plethora of medical interventions in the form of hip replacements, knee replacements and back surgeries, but why then is it that one hip wears out and not both at the same time? What is it that causes some joints to wear out and others not?

The answer lies in loads (*see* Chapter 1) and more specifically the loads you apply to your joints by the way you move, the way you position your body and the movement habits that you have adopted over your lifetime. The body does a great job in keeping you moving but it cannot continue to shorten, lengthen and pass off the loads to another structure if you ask it the same question each and every day for sixty or more years. Loads have the potential to change the shape of your bones, so if you constantly load one leg differently from the other, the bones are going to be affected differently. If you have osteoarthritis in a hip, you will have loaded that leg with forces on the soft tissues which have pulled the bones closer together, rotated them and kept them locked in place, which over time has created friction – heat – which ends in osteoarthritis. The body is responding constantly to the sensations it receives from the environment, and this includes how it interacts with the environment all the time. If you always walk with one foot turned out whilst the other one points straight ahead, the loads experienced by the knees and hips will be completely different. It is this that affects the health of your joints much more than the natural demise of tissues that comes with age.

So what does this mean? The good news is that, armed with the right information and the right tools, you are able to make positive changes to how you experience your advancing years. The saying 'If you don't use it, you lose it' is very true, but it can equally be said that 'If you use it too much, you will lose it'. Load is incredibly powerful; if you change the loads you place on your body, you can change the effect they have, which is likely to change how you feel, move and ride.

YOUR NORMAL BASE OF SUPPORT

Any time you don't outsource your movement responsibility to a chair (and you are not in the saddle), the point of contact for force to enter the body is at foot level. How this force is experienced further up the body is dependent upon how the foot is able to interact with the ground.

FOOTWEAR

Your feet are probably not the body part you would choose to pay much attention to, but showing them some biomechanical love might just change your world – or your body, at least. In Chapter 2 we saw how the feet were designed to interact with the ground, how they were a strong and dextrous part of the body and how significant they are to your entire biomechanical story.

APPEARANCES CAN BE DECEPTIVE

It is not all about how you look in the saddle. Some of the best-positioned riders in the world carry pain and dysfunction in their bodies and some of the most talented horses are working from a place of significant tension and compensatory patterns of movement. For both parties, the aim always has to be to move the body away from pain and back to alignment and sustainable function. This is the best outcome for you and your horse, whatever riding aspirations you may have.

The modern-day story of the foot is incredibly different. Society is plagued with foot pain from bunions, corns, plantar fasciitis, toe pain and heel pain, with orthotics being a common addition to many shoes. Modern living requires that we wear some sort of footwear all the time. It is not safe to walk on the pavement in bare feet, let alone to the stables, and it would be largely socially unacceptable to turn up to work with no shoes on. However, it is this constant casting of the feet within shoes, preventing the feet moving or interacting with the ground, that creates this chronic level of foot pain and changes the way the entire body is able to move.

Most shoes have similar features, which include thick soles, a small area for the toes and a positive heel (where the heel is higher than the toe). In the fitness space, plenty of work and research has been put into making shoes as comfortable as possible for the wearer, whilst providing an ergonomic benefit. Typically soles have become thicker with concussive-reducing gel inserts, arch supports or technology that can be moulded to support your tendency to over- or under-pronate. The upper portion of the shoe tends to be fairly rigid to provide decent 'support' to the foot. In essence, the shoe is trying to be smarter than the engineering of the foot. Outside sport, there are a plethora of shoe types for fashion, leisure and work. Many of these require you to hold them on with your toes, or have a very narrow space for the toes, or have a thick sole and high heels. All of these factors will affect how the foot is able to function, how it is loaded and the shape it becomes.

CASTING YOUR FEET

'Casting' a body part, such as putting feet in shoes, is the same as putting a cast on a broken bone. When the cast comes off, your leg or arm looks really small and weak. The tissues have not been used, so have atrophied (cell death). This is what happens to feet that live in shoes.

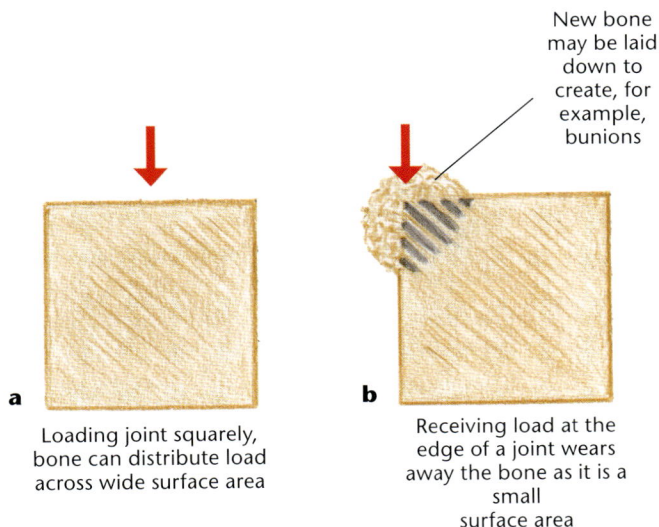

New bone may be laid down to create, for example, bunions

a Loading joint squarely, bone can distribute load across wide surface area

b Receiving load at the edge of a joint wears away the bone as it is a small surface area

Fig. 29   Loading joints squarely.
a) Joints are designed to be loaded squarely so there is a larger surface area to distribute the load.
b) When the joints are loaded from a position of misalignment, the load affects only the edge of the bone. This leads to damage and, in the case of bunions on the feet, the body will lay down new bone to protect the damaged area from the loads it is receiving.

Shoes reduce the amount of movement the structures of the foot will experience. Once again, we outsource our innate movement requirement to something artificial. Where once your foot would have read, absorbed and interacted with the ground, now shoes carry you across the ground in various degrees of cushioned comfort.

Over-pronation: a common problem

Your feet are connected to your ankle, your ankle is connected to your shin bone, your shin bone is connected to your thigh bone and at the top of your thigh bone is your hip. The point is that what is happening further up your leg will have an impact on what happens at ground level, and vice versa. In the case of over-pronation of the foot (where the foot rolls to the inside), the problem has started at the top of the leg. When the muscles on the outside of the hip are weak, the hip is free to rotate inwards as there is not enough muscular strength to keep it facing forwards. This brings the thigh bone (femur) inwards, which affects the positioning of the bones all the way down the leg and the inside of the foot ends up sliding down towards the floor. Walking with this posture can create pain in the foot and the ankle. The shape of the foot normally gets the blame, so corrective orthotics are often prescribed. Unfortunately this simply adjusts the positioning of the foot artificially without strengthening the frame it is attached to. This impacts the rider's position in the saddle, as described in Chapter 4.

POSITIVE HEELED FOOTWEAR

If you have ever had a high heel hangover, you will know that your body has to make some adjustments when you wear serious leg-lengthening shoes, but what you may not know is that however high the heel is, if it is higher than the toe of your shoe by even half an inch, the entire geometry of your body has to change to keep you upright and prevent you from falling forwards. The degree to which the whole body can be displaced by positive heeled shoes can be significant. It will relate to the height of the heel, but any amount of geometrical change will have physical and biological repercussions.

Fig. 30 shows how a heel tips the body forward onto the toes. Remaining in this position would cause you to fall over, so to avoid that, and to appear upright, your body has to displace parts and take them out of alignment. This catastrophic adjustment normally has to occur at the level of the lumbar spine and pelvis, but your exact change of geometry will be unique to you (depending on your movement habits, the anatomy of your body parts, injuries and so on). What has to happen is the same in everybody; although the extent or impact that it has on your own body may be different from what happens in other people, the fundamentals remain the same.

In order to appear (and to stay) upright with the weight forced onto the toes, you must lean your shoulders back and thrust your pelvis forward (see Fig. 30). This immediately removes the ability of your hips to move into extension and puts extra stress over your knees; your ankles are hovering above the ground and the area of ground reaction force (toes only) is really small. This all adds up to limited stability, limited intelligence (proprioception), stiff ankles and joints that are being loaded incorrectly (the knees are taking too much, the hips not taking enough). The lower back is forced into extension, the glutes are not activated to bring the hip into extension, so the sacro-iliac joint is unsupported. Walking in this position each day and sitting with the ankles off the floor under the desk will change the length of the muscles

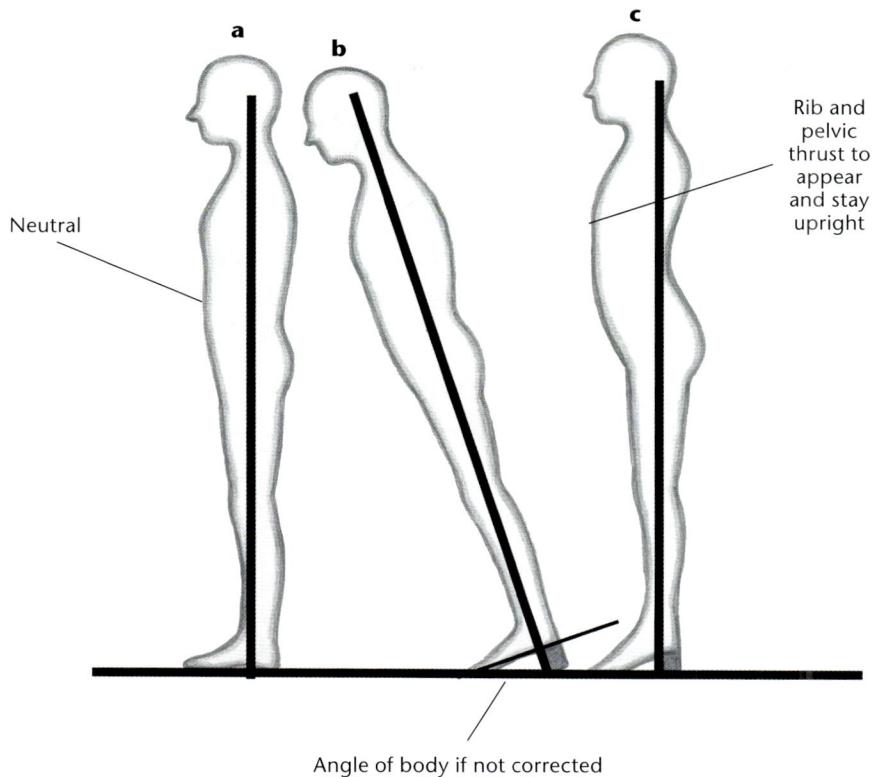

Neutral

Rib and pelvic thrust to appear and stay upright

Angle of body if not corrected

Fig. 30   Positive heeled footwear.
a)   This shows a body in neutral position, without positive heeled footwear.
b)   The position the body would be in when wearing heeled shoes if it didn't make any adjustments to stay upright. The height of the heel determines the angle of displacement of the body.
c)   The adjustments the body has to make; notice the pelvic tilt and rib thrust.

in your calves, glutes, lower back and around the hips.

ANKLE OSCILLATION

All of this foot casting in shoes affects the function not only of the foot, but of the ankle too (after all, the foot bones are connected to the ankle bones). So when the foot within a shoe is unable to roll over terrain, this job is moved to the ankle, which is the next movable point above the foot. The problem the ankle faces is that it does not receive enough input from the foot about where it is in time and space; communications are blurred by the shoe. Without this information, the ankle is vulnerable to movement, so it tries not to move too much. This leaves the ligaments weak, so when you walk on uneven terrain or step in a hole, the ankle has no infrastructure to keep the bones aligned, and typically you end up spraining your ankle. The problem then is that you stretch the ligaments, leaving them lax, so the chances are you never just sprain your ankle once.

ARE PROFESSIONAL RIDERS IMMUNE TO PAIN AND DYSFUNCTION?

If you are not a professional rider it might be tempting to assume that they are operating with brilliantly functioning bodies, but the truth is that they too suffer from pain and dysfunction. The real issue is that no one has been taught how to move and we have lost the lifestyle that led us into natural movement.

Professional riders have bodies that are well adapted to riding; they have strength, technique and balance, and they have good proprioceptive responses because the stimuli are so familiar. But it is still not a varied movement environment for the body. Loading sequences will rarely be challenged, different areas of the body will not be utilized and joints will be cast in the same positions for most of the day. This means they are vulnerable to new or different movements and are prone to the same issues as any other body that goes through repetitive geometry.

Why is this relevant?

Studies have shown that riders with an improved seat and loading/absorption ability in sitting trot absorb much more movement through flexible ankles than riders who cannot absorb or synchronize the movements in their joints with those of the horse. The ankle has been proven to be a key part of this technique.

It is not possible to affect the foot and ignore the ankle; what happens to each affects the other. When the foot is unable to roll over the ground, then the ankle does it instead. In an ideal, aligned world we would all walk with our feet facing straight ahead, like properly aligned wheels on a car travelling on a straight piece of road. This allows the foot and ankle to work within their biomechanic happy place; the bodyweight is taken onto the heel as the first phase, then transferred via the sole to be rolled forward over the big toe in a straight line. The joints of the foot are all loaded squarely, so there is no presence of bunions or corns.

When the ankle and foot are moved in this way the bones of the ankle joint are stacked correctly and the ligaments receive load in

the right direction for them to strengthen. Remember, only joints that feel strong enough to move are able to absorb shock – in other words, strong joints will be mobile. Weak joints will be stiff and vulnerable to changes in load.

A healthy foot and ankle complex should cope brilliantly even with a rabbit hole or a divot. The foot will receive stimuli from the uneven terrain and will inform the brain that an adjustment must be made or the body is likely to fall. The ankle, its own computer of all things in time and space, makes the necessary adjustment in positioning; maybe it has had to move the bones into a shearing position to accommodate the loss of ground, but with strong ligaments it is able to correct the momentum before it goes too far.

The ligaments of the ankle joint can be thought of as springs: a stretched spring cannot absorb shock, and neither can one that is tightly compressed.

TRAUMA AND INJURY

It is very rare to get through a horse-filled life without encountering any injuries or traumas to the body. It is likely that you will have bones that are a bit bent out of shape, or soft tissues that are not as complete as they once were, and maybe you have some man-made materials holding you together in some places. Your body might not have everything in the perfect position, and it may not function completely how it should. My own is a story of so much crookedness you get lost on your way from start to finish. Your body is meant to be lived in, and no rider would profess to have one that is perfectly symmetrical or aligned or completely functioning. However, the body you do have can probably be made a little bit better, just by your being aware of how you are moving. Injuries and trauma are inevitable, but your body has a high level of functional tolerance so it will adapt and allow you to keep going. But the important thing is that small, mindful movement which supports how your body copes with areas that might not be perfect is critical to giving you and your horse a more comfortable and successful ride.

4 The Riding Connection

'Your body wants to be aligned, strong and mobile. And your horse wants it to be, too.'

Debbie Rolmanis

Riding is the only sport where two different brain-body systems are asked to merge and to work synergistically with each other. From a movement perspective it would appear completely irrational to put horse and rider together, yet despite an understandable level of difficulty, we know that it can, and does, work.

In every sport your skill level increases with the time spent learning, refining and building sensory input. Riding is no exception. The best way to improve your skill level for riding is through riding, but to build a complete athlete the body needs to be prepared in the best way to be able to learn the skills required. A tennis player may have an amazing forehand, but if his body can't get him to the ball when he is on court, his skill in hitting the ball means nothing. Improving the way you ride comes from preparing the body so that it is ready to learn the technical skill of riding when you are in the saddle. The idea that 'practice makes perfect' has the correct premise at its core, but you can practise riding with a body that is out of alignment for as many hours as you like and all you will do is strengthen the imbalance. Improvement, in the form of soundness, welfare and performance, can only come from a place of alignment, awareness and an understanding of the rules of movement.

Typically, riders spend more of their time working on attaining the skills required for riding than preparing the body to be ready to learn those skills. The notion of treating riders as athletes is only really beginning to take hold in the amateur section of the sport but let it be known that if you ride a horse, you are an athlete and you should be preparing your body as an athlete would.

As a rider you face a unique set of challenges not encountered by athletes in other sports. Not only do you have to learn the technique for a training system, you have to get your body into a position to implement that technique and then synchronize what you do with how your horse moves.

The collision between horse and rider attempting to move in harmony sets the stage for injury, pain and poor performance, and the heartbreak over this fact of riding life has not sidestepped any rider, at any level. The journey into riding is one of constant learning, so there will be times when you will not always enable the horse to move brilliantly, and similarly, whilst the horse is learning and strengthening he will find it hard to always support you in the most balanced way. As soon as one part of the team starts to reduce his movement performance, the partner athlete is affected. If the rider is out of alignment and therefore not balanced, or has weak postural control or is stiff through the joints or is in pain, the horse will change how he moves, compromising his own musculo-skeletal health. A horse compensating in his movement will mean that crookedness is increased, creating a ripple effect through the horse's body, and it becomes much harder for the rider to control. A rider who has the ability to not be negatively influenced by a horse's way of going is able to help that horse to learn how to move his body in a better, more sustainable and comfortable way, but this is only achieved if the rider is body aware, has a body which can physically get into the right position and has a balanced level of strength and mobility. These attributes are rarely achieved just from riding; as you have seen, the way you are moving all the time is responsible for the body you bring to the saddle and therefore what that body *does* in the saddle.

The training journey of horse and rider is fraught with difficulties. There is an endless list of training maladies that plague every single rider at some point: a horse behind the leg, heavy in the contact, rushing, head tilting, leaning in, wrong canter strike off, head in the air, head on the ground. At the core of all these problems (where pain has been ruled out) is a lack of balance, which stems directly from a lack of alignment from both horse and rider (individually and together). A rider who is out of alignment within their own body will (unintentionally) force the horse to move or behave in a way that does not advance his training. The training issues many riders experience are often down to their horse hustling underneath their unbalanced position

in order to meet his innate need to stay balanced enough to remain on his feet.

Both horse and rider rely on balance in order to move in a way that is biomechanically suitable for their respective bodies, but both are imperfect beings; riders will always be asymmetrical and horses, although to a lesser extent than riders, will always want to be crooked and they have to learn a way of going that is not entirely natural. Riding well is about managing the imbalances of both in a way that impacts both parties in the least damaging way.

Many riders have regular lessons; their drive to improve their horse's way of going and performance whilst learning to be more effective are motivators that solidify a consistent amount of effort. Unfortunately, many postural and positional corrections that are made in the saddle can easily spiral into increased tension and crookedness, which limits the rider's ability to make the changes the coach is trying to see and that they are trying to achieve. Occasionally, the correction that is called for can appear to make an aesthetic difference but more often than not this difference is not relative to the rider's body as a whole and only serves to add another layer

SHORT-TERM VS LONG-TERM FIXES

Many short-term 'fixes' in rider positioning act as a metaphorical sticking plaster. You can cover something up for a short time, but the problem is still there. This is definitely the case for rider performance. Proficiency in anything does not happen overnight. Short-term fixes are just that: short-term. They may last for the duration of a lesson but, without awareness, understanding and the ability to replicate, riders will not improve their position simply because they had an instructor telling them to put their shoulders back or turn their toes forwards. The illusion that progress has been made quickly seduces coaches all the time, but the same lesson has to be taught over and over again. The long game takes more consideration, more understanding and a desire to put in the work that is required. For the rider, this involves moving and getting the body into a good shape on the ground so that positional corrections in the saddle become cues rather than contortions.

of dysfunction to the rider's body. Making large corrections to a rider's position in the saddle is often too late. A rider with a pelvis that sits out of neutral all day will not be able to sit in neutral in the saddle. This means that their leg position is not going to be correct. A rider who has too much tension in the hips all day probably will not be able to keep their feet facing forward in the stirrup (at least not for the duration of the ride). Finding out how your position can be improved from the way you move on the ground gives you an amazing tool kit, because it means you can be working on your position wherever you are.

In order to address some of the most common rider faults, it is first necessary to take a look at some horse biomechanics because, as you have seen, the way you ride will influence how your horse is able to move. Knowing how your horse should move allows you to paint a clearer picture of how you can interact with him in a more suitable way. There is also a third companion to your riding story and that is your saddle, which is the interface between you and your horse. The saddle is the platform for your body to perform on, and it has a major influence on how you sit and therefore how your horse can move. Regular saddle fitting is a must for every horse and rider combination, to make sure that you are connecting to your horse through something that supports a balanced seat and does not impinge on how your horse is able to move. Horse, rider and saddle interaction is a topic that requires a lot more research, so for the purpose of this book it is assumed that all you are bringing to the horse is your own asymmetry and not that of the saddle.

BIOMECHANICS OF THE HORSE: AN OUTLINE

As prey animals, horses have an inbuilt desire and motivation to stay upright, so they position their bodies over their limbs in a way that ensures they are safe from falling over. In an ideal biomechanical world for a horse, he would be required only to move in a straight line. It would be very unusual to see a wild horse try to escape a predator by cantering in small circles. The horse's body evolved to graze, gallop and walk/trot in straight lines to new places for food and water. As a quadruped, he is able to swing his vast ribcage and abdominal contents from side to side when needed to maintain balance. He also uses his head and neck in various positions to shift his balance over his front or hind legs, as needed, dependent upon the terrain.

The horse did not evolve to take weight/load directly on his back. Biomechanically, the back was designed to be stabilized by broad, large muscles in order to counteract the weight beneath it of the abdominal mass and gravitational pull. The natural posture of a horse in the wild is to spend ten to twelve hours a day with his head lowered to graze. This position activates a mechanical pulley style system via the strong nuchal ligament that runs from the poll to the sacrum and has attachments to the vertebral column. When this ligament is under traction (when the neck is lowered), it helps to support the weight of the head and neck and invokes a flexion of the entire spine, which then recruits the multifidi (the same stabilizers as in people) and triggers an increase in work from the abdominals.

The horse's back is a matrix of broad, strong and dense muscles that between them have both a stabilizing function and a movement role. The muscles of the abdomen by comparison are far less substantial. This would suggest that the muscles of the back are designed to both flex and stabilize the spine, with some support from the abdominal group, but the abdominals are not responsible for purely creating spinal flexion or spinal support. The back is the key player for both horse and rider in terms of biomechanical health, balance, comfort and performance.

In order to provide the horse with the right movement environment to be able to carry a rider comfortably, it is essential that he is worked in a way that complements his natural biomechanic as much as possible. Having the head and neck in a position that applies traction to the ligaments above the spine has been accepted as good riding and training practice for decades. The aim must be to strengthen and create tone in the muscles of the back and the entire 'top line' (the muscles that sit above the skeleton from the poll to the tail). In human movement, lengthening the spine and applying loads and postures that encourage the spine to be decompressed is the focus for a healthy vertebral column. The same is true for your horse. The traction and lengthening just happens on a horizontal plane rather than a vertical one. This means that for your horse to move more comfortably and support the weight of a rider, his back needs to be under traction and this happens from contact at the front of the body (into the hand) and a loading of the hindquarters.

If you consider the horse's muscular system to be like an elastic band, and you want to apply a stretch to the band, you need to load it at both ends, and this is what has to happen for the horse to work correctly. In this state, the vertebrae are stabilized through their position and subsequent activation of their deep stabilizers (the multifidi), allowing the larger, more superficial muscles to move through contraction and lengthening, enabling the back to behave like a trampoline underneath the rider. Posturally, this lifting of the back activates a lifting of the abdomen, which gives space for the hind leg to step underneath the belly. The magnitude of effort from the abdominals will depend on how much hind limb engagement there is, and this will relate in part to how the psoas muscle is able to flex the lumbar spine. In the horse, this muscle also

attaches the lumbar spine to the thigh, helping to 'tuck' the hindquarters underneath the body. Only when the muscles of the horse's back are healthy and the spine is held in the right posture are these powerful muscles kept at the right length to contract and bring the hind legs underneath when increased amounts of loading and collection are required.

Structures need to be loaded in order to strengthen so the neck/shoulders and chest should carry and lift some load, but the balance has to be such that these structures are not overloaded. It is not about throwing the head and neck low and leaving the horse to carry all of his weight on his forehand. He will naturally want to take 60 per cent of his weight on the front half of his body, but the aim is not to burden the forelimbs with this much effort. The aim of true top-line stretch, which elicits correct spinal flexion, spacious vertebrae and abdominal activity, is to draw the horse into an elastic contact via hind leg engagement, where energy travels along the top of the body through a soft base of the neck and into the hand. Only through working in this position will sufficient strength be created along the top of the neck, withers and underneath the rider to be able to maintain this lengthening when the head and neck are brought into a higher position. Typically, the nuchal ligament system is slackened when the head and neck are lifted and, if the horse has not learnt how to keep drawing across the top line, when the posture of his head and neck is changed to come higher, he will have to do it through muscular tension, which will render the spinal support system useless. In this scenario the vertebrae can become too close together and in some cases can impinge on each other (a problem known as kissing spines). In this position the horse only has one choice and that is to apply a bracing mechanism to the muscles of his back in an attempt to stabilize and minimize any further downward movement of the spine. With this hollow, stiff back, the heavy contents of the abdomen succumb to the pull of gravity and apply a downward loading force to the spine, further encouraging it to collapse and requiring the back muscles to create even more tension to support the weight of the rider.

The position – and consequent state – of the muscles of the horse's back is enormously significant to how the horse can move, and how sound and comfortable he will be, because it is through the back that the hindquarters are connected to the front of the body, and of course it is the back of the horse that the rider interacts with most directly.

To be biomechanically sound, the push from the hindquarters of the horse must be able to be transmitted to the forehand and this can only be done through a back that has good muscular tone, enabling it to absorb and synthesize the forces it receives via the hind legs and pelvis. A vertebral column that is not supported will be surrounded by muscles in a high state of tension; as you know from learning about your own body, tension means that the muscle is weak. In this scenario the muscles are unable to cope with the forces from the hindquarters and, with the belly dropped, the horse has no choice but to keep his hind legs out behind him and use them like pogo sticks. As you will see when sitting trot is discussed, this creates a springboard type of feeling in the muscles of the back rather than the desired trampoline effect. The result of this action may be shown at the front of the horse through a display of discomfort, inconsistencies into the contact, and a bracing of the neck. The forehand runs into increasing amounts of trouble as it is forced to take more load. In an attempt to protect the shoulder girdle, the muscles of the pectorals, base of the neck and shoulder will brace to protect the body and to provide enough force to push back against the ground with. The entire muscular system is unable to absorb the forces created with each step, leaving joints crashing into each other and setting the scene for damage and injury.

HORSE, RIDER AND SADDLE INTERACTION

There are many aspects to horse and rider performance, and the most significant in the context of this book is the relationship between the horse, the rider and the saddle as the interface between the two. It is always necessary to look at each component separately; the horse will bring his own postural imbalances to the relationship, just as the rider does, but how these two meet is influenced by how the saddle fits both parties. For example, how the saddle interacts laterally with the horse can be responsible for a rider sitting in a crooked position, while a tree that is too wide can influence the position of the rider's pelvis. It is therefore critical to become aware of the rider's natural positioning off-horse, the horse's own postural tendencies and how the saddle needs to be fitted to support each one. The importance of working with a team cannot be underestimated.

THE SIGNIFICANCE OF STRAIGHTNESS

When we talk about alignment, or straightness, what we are indirectly referring to is balance. The idea that the body needs to be balanced over its base of support means that each side of the body takes an even distribution of load. In the horse, a quadruped, there are four quarters to balance with load, and the neck and head make a fifth. With people on two legs, the balance points are less complex: are you standing more on one leg than the other?

Horses, like humans, are naturally asymmetrical and this sets up a cycle of uneven loading of the limbs. Horses all have a dominant foreleg; just as children naturally lean towards using their right or left hand when they start to draw/write/play, horses have a one-sided tendency that can be seen in foals as they graze. Foals habitually place one foreleg out in front of them as a strut to lean over, whilst keeping the other foreleg back underneath the body. This asymmetry creates different loads through the two front limbs and sets up a cycle of laterality throughout the body. Working with hundreds of horses, this pattern of a dominant foreleg that wanted to carry load, leaving the other foreleg to push the body over the ground showed up time and again.

Let's take a look. Imagine for a moment that your horse is right fore dominant; therefore his right fore is a CARRYING limb, having been loaded with more weight out in front of the body from a foal. The hoof capsule is likely to be a different size, as there will be more weight on the heel of this hoof, leaving it lower and flatter. The left fore will have more weight on the toe of the foot and less on the heel, so it will have more of an upright shape. The left fore is a PUSHING limb, pushing the body over the ground and towards the carrying forelimb. Working through the body, the horse has diagonal slings of muscular connection, just as you do, which dictates the role of each hind leg. The left hind (diagonal to the right fore) takes on the role of a pushing limb, as it will want to push the body over the right fore. The right hind then has to be a carrying limb.

What will this feel like under saddle?

As the dominant foreleg, the right fore will naturally be happier to be under load away from the midline of the body. If you have ridden a horse that goes more easily one way than the other, this is why.

Imagine you are trotting a circle on the left rein on the right fore-dominant horse. You will likely feel that he draws into your outside rein and gives you the feeling of good inside 'bend'. This is because his right fore is happy to carry more weight and will move towards the outside of the circle (away from the body).

Take the same horse onto a circle on the right rein and you will feel him leaning in, not giving you enough bend and not drawing into your outside rein.

Why?

The explanation is that he wants to carry more load on his dominant foreleg and the left side of his body is pushing his bodyweight onto it. To stay upright, he has to move the dominant foreleg to the inside of the circle to catch the body.

In the hind limbs, it is common for the right hind to look weaker, with slightly less muscle tone in the glutes and a bit slower off the ground. This is understandable if you consider that it is a carrying limb, not a pushing limb. It does not need as much strength to propel the horse forward, but rather has to provide a strut of support, which means it will be on the ground a little longer but will not necessarily build as many pushing muscles as the left hind.

All of this would be fine if the horse was not expected to carry a rider, or jump fences, or canter in a small circle, but the tasks asked of the modern horse's body demand that the way the limbs are loaded is equalized if any sustainable level of skill attainment, comfort and soundness is going to occur.

Straightness in the horse means that each side of his body is taking the same amount of load. There is a lot of literature around the natural balance of the horse from front to back, but how the horse uses himself from side to side is less often considered. The aim must be to achieve an even job share of carrying and pushing from both hind legs into an even contact, so that the loading of horse and rider is distributed evenly across the limbs on the left and those on the right.

This load share is critical if you are going to avoid injuries to the limbs that occur through overloading, which happens when the horse is not moving straight. Working the horse in his natural configuration of push and carry, you can quite easily see that the load share is not even. This continual uneven overloading of limbs can set the stage for damage and injury, so it is really important to straighten the horse by getting the dominant foreleg under control and back underneath the body. If you imagine springs running across the horse diagonally, connecting his hind legs to his forehand, you will see that the placement of each corner of the horse's body has an effect on the other end of the spring. Only when the horse has his weight balanced from side to side can these slings be strengthened evenly, which explains why you can only achieve true connection from the hindquarters to the forehand, across the top line, when the horse is straight.

Alignment in the horse refers to the stacking of body segments in a horizontal plane (as opposed to a vertical one). This means the shoulders must be in front of the hindquarters and the ribs should stay in line with the shoulders. When a horse is moved in alignment, both hind legs have the opportunity to take equal amounts of load, which means their ground reaction force will be similar, so the loads through the pelvis and into the back will be more even. Having loads that are even on the left and right sides means that the muscles receive a similar amount of force and can therefore work in a more symmetrical fashion.

THE CYCLE OF CROOKEDNESS

Crookedness means that the horse is not loading his body evenly because his body is not aligned and his dominant foreleg has set up the cycle of push and carry through the limbs that has gone unchecked. Working the horse in this way sets up a cycle of crookedness, beginning with:

spinal rotation: as with people, horses always want to keep their eyes level. When there is an alignment problem through the body, the spine will rotate left and right the entire way from poll to tail. Imagine you are twisting a towel to wring it out: this is what the spine does to compensate for an imbalance of push and carry. This creates:

an **imbalance of muscular tension**: overloaded muscles become dysfunctional and sit alongside underused and weak muscles, creating an imbalance of **tension**. This creates:

an **imbalance of joint mobility**: muscles are responsible for moving bones from one position to another. Bones are able to move because of movable joints. Where an imbalance of muscular tension affects a bone, the joint is not fully supported and will therefore reduce its mobility to protect itself. This creates:

an **inability to be supple**: joints that do not move through their full range of movement are stiff, not supple. Can't get inside bend? Your horse cannot be supple until he is straight. This creates:

SKILL VS BIOMECHANICS

When the training of a skill/movement ignores the non-negotiables of biomechanics, the horse suffers from negative mechanical input. Working in this way means that every step is a step closer to injury.

whole body tension: when individual joints are unable to move correctly, the whole system has to compensate. A body in compensation mode is full of negative tension. This creates:

damage to vulnerable structures: tendons, ligaments, cartilage and vertebrae. Tension means structures are unable to cope with the LOAD they are expected to carry. Wear and tear, strains and inflammation will arise. This creates:

pain: this is usually the first stage at which we may become aware that the horse has been in trouble; it normally first manifests as a loss of performance and/or undesirable behaviour. This creates:

further muscular imbalance: as soon as the horse feels pain, more soft tissues will switch off, taking the body further into the cycle of imbalance and compensation. This creates:

instability of vertebrae and joints: setting the scene for injury and lameness.

Thus the need for straightness training cannot be underestimated.

WHERE CROOKEDNESS COLLIDES

Merging horse and rider is a challenge, and one of the biggest aspects involves bringing together two asymmetric bodies to try to create one unit of straightness. Riders typically carry more crookedness within their bodies than horses do, so if you add a rider who sits with more weight on one side of their seat, pulls more with one hand, grips or pushes more with one leg, on top of a horse who is carrying his own pattern of push and carry and uneven loading, the cycle of crookedness becomes inescapable. The horse's limbs do not have an indefinite loading life in them. It is thought that the loading cycle of each limb is 10,000 steps before it breaks down. If your horse travels crookedly, loading one limb with more weight than another, or if you sit crookedly and therefore load one limb more than another, that limb won't reach 10,000 steps. When considering loads and force, it is necessary to consider the increases in forces from the rider's mass as the gait speed increases. By the time you get to canter, the loads your horse has to manage are two and a half times your bodyweight. If you add into this any uneven weight distribution of your seat in the saddle, your horse will have to compensate to make sure you do not pull him off balance. This means he will have to travel crookedly, which means he has to load his limbs unevenly, so he won't be straight and his back will not be supported by top line traction, and he will have to try to cope with the increase in downward force onto a braced back. This gives you that springboard feeling, making it difficult to sit on, and the spiral of imbalance becomes fairly severe. With this knowledge, teaching your horse how to balance his limbs and draw through the top line correctly should be done in walk, and only once the technique is achieved in walk should you ask the horse to trot and so on.

The good news in all of this is that you are in control of what your body does. It might mean

WHAT MAKES A GREAT RIDER?

The ability to consistently coordinate the positioning of their own and their horse's centre of gravity.

that you have to retrain your body's movement on the ground and work continuously off-horse to move in alignment, to mobilize and to strengthen, but what you bring to the saddle – and therefore burden the horse with – is within your control. Having an awareness of what your body is doing, and what your horse's body is doing, is key to building a sound and sustainable team of athletes. It is vital to understand that the crookedness of your horse is his attempt, in the only way he knows how, to stay upright. It is up to you, as his rider, to give him the best environment to balance the push and carry of his limbs, to identify the dominant foreleg and to bring it back underneath his body, to manage his steps so that he takes more aligned and building ones than crooked and destructive ones, and to allow his body to work in a way that enables him to support you on his back without having to resort to tension.

ALIGNMENT AND CENTRE OF GRAVITY

If we were to compare professional riders with amateurs, we would see a range of aesthetic differences – both in the rider's position and in how the horse moves. The main reason for this is how much postural control the rider has over their position, and how much influence the horse's way of going has on the rider.

Riding means you have to balance a vertical centre of gravity with a horizontal centre of gravity and the position of the two is in constant flow. It changes with gait and speed within the gait, and is influenced by any asymmetry or crooked patterns of positioning that the horse and rider may have singularly and together.

The centres of gravity of horse and rider also move relative to each other; this means the horse will be affected by where the

NEUROMUSCULAR DEVELOPMENT OF THE RIDER/MOTOR CONTROL

As you saw in Chapter 2, your core has an inbuilt proprioceptive ability to respond via reflex to the position the body and limbs are in. This system can become really sluggish if the body is not moved well during the day, but in a body that functions well (and this has been developed in elite riders) their core proprioception enables them to appear very still and poised in the saddle whilst it is taking care of all the sensory input it is receiving from the horse's movement.

The development of motor control for riding develops with learning and training, but knowing that the body is going to be subjected to copious amounts of stimuli when on-horse, you can prepare the body to become more accustomed to stimuli by changing your movement habits. Outsourcing movement does not just affect you on a mechanical level; it affects the way your body interacts with the world around you and this applies to how it is going to receive the movement stimulus provided by riding.

Elite riders are quicker to adapt to a reaction from their horse, whether this is a subtle movement stimulus or a great big spook. This is only possible if the entire core unit is strong and mobile and the body's proprioceptive receptors within the muscles of the core and around the joints have a clear and unhindered pathway to the brain. This can only happen if the muscles and joints are healthy through correct strengthening and mobility.

rider's centre of gravity is. As the rider, you are a load for your horse, and how you sit and where you sit in the saddle changes how he has to carry you. It is the same as if you were to carry a bag of horse feed over one shoulder or cradled in front of you; the weight has not changed but the way it is loading your body has. The position you hold in the saddle affects the entirety of your horse's body, and every positional misalignment creates a whole new load for him to deal with.

CENTRE OF GRAVITY

The centre of gravity relates to the point at which gravity has the most effect on your

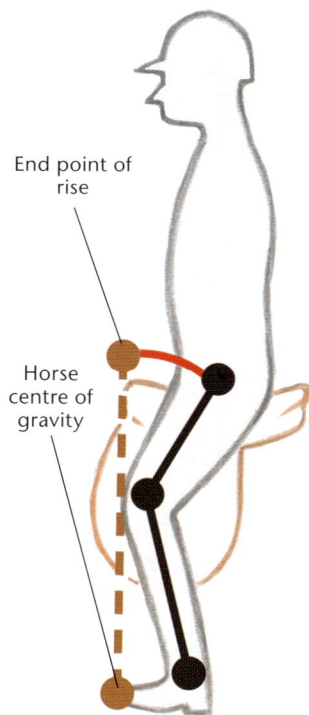

body. It is also sometimes referred to as the centre of mass. When this centre is within your base of support, you will feel balanced. When this point moves away from your base of support, you lose balance and are more likely to fall over.

Good alignment in the saddle, with the pelvis in neutral and shoulder, hip and heel in line.

End point of rise

Horse centre of gravity

Neutral
Optimal length of arc of rise. Rider is in balance with horse

This shows a rider in alignment with the horse's centre of gravity because her pelvis is in neutral, and the arc of the rising trot.

Another example of good alignment in the saddle, with a neutral pelvis.

Riding means that your base of support moves from your feet to your pelvis, but we also need to consider the significance of your horse being a part of your base of support. Riding 'in balance' means that you have to coordinate the positioning of your centre of gravity with that of your horse.

Your own centre of gravity will depend on your body shape: length of spine, length of legs, weight and concentration of weight (in other words, where you carry it). This is true for your position both in and out of the saddle. For the purposes of this book, consider everything that happens from your torso to your thighs as having the potential to either combine your centre of gravity with that of

your horse, or to separate them. As a general rule, your standing centre of mass (or gravity) is about 10cm lower than your navel. This is going to alter when you sit on a horse, as it will when you move the position of your arms or your upper body.

To illustrate the significance of your centre of gravity, let's take a look at a universal challenge: the rising trot. With the rider in an aligned position, imagine that the horse's centre of gravity is in a vertical line with the rider's knee. In this scenario, the rider is working with the horse's centre of gravity below her knee. Her pelvis is level and her seatbones have a horizontal positioning and even load. When she rises, her hips will be

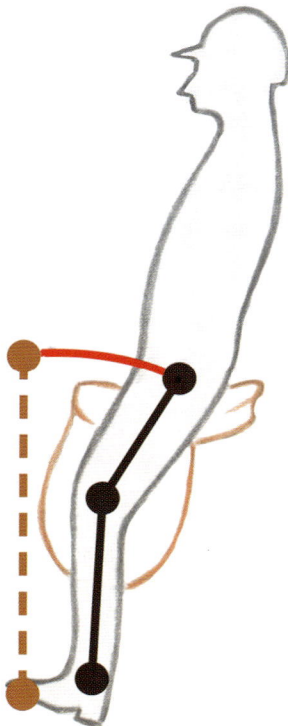

This shows a rider with their CoG behind that of the horse. Notice the longer arc required in rising trot.

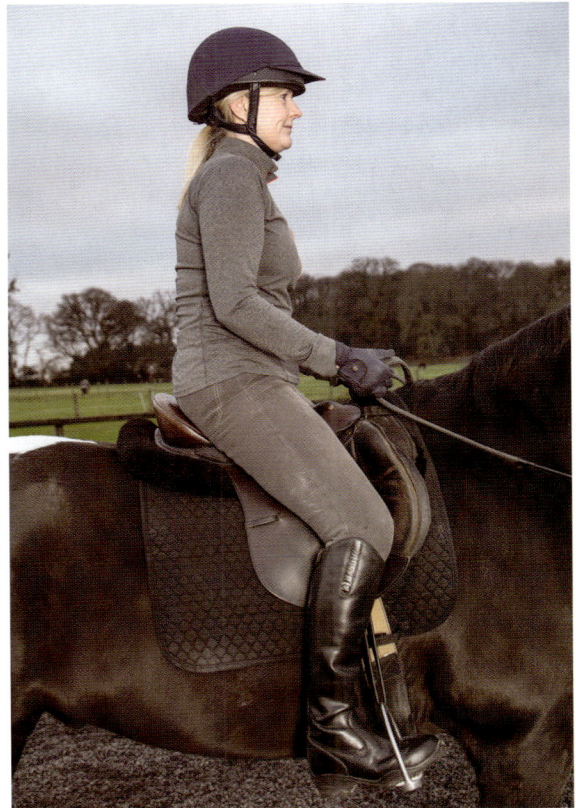

Posterior Tilt
Longer arc of rise, rider will be behind the movement. Horse will slow down to move CoG back towards the rider

This rider has moved her centre of gravity behind that of the horse, because her pelvis is in a posterior tilt, and as such will be behind the movement.

above her knee and she will make a consistent arc with the line of her pelvis as she rises and sits. In both the rising and sitting phases of the trot she will stay over the horse's centre of gravity, which will move with each stride to stay under hers.

In the second scenario, we have a rider who has a biomechanic of a tucked or posterior tilted pelvis, which takes her upper body behind the hip. This moves her centre of gravity further backwards, behind her knee, and therefore behind where the horse might choose to have it.

With the pelvis in this position, the seat bones are now sitting in front of the hip joints, which has the effect of pushing the horse's head and neck lower and placing his centre of gravity over the shoulders. This position creates a larger arc that the pelvis has to travel to 'catch up' with the horse's centre of gravity, and the rider has to work harder to rise and get out of the saddle. This increased distance inevitably puts the rider 'behind the movement' as she has pushed the horse's balance point further forward, but she is sitting further behind it. Her centre of gravity is moving away from her base of support (her pelvis) so she will be out of balance. What then happens is she will try to hold herself upright with the reins, or grip on with the legs. From the horse's point of view, this lack of congruency between the centres of gravity is not ideal; he too needs his own centre of gravity to be within his base of support and when the rider influences it negatively, he will try to remedy things. The only achievable solution he has is to adjust his speed and/or stride length. In this instance, he will slow his speed to try to bring his centre of gravity closer to being in line with the rider's. The rider then finds herself wanting to kick with every stride, or use spurs or a whip to get the horse 'in front of her leg', as she believes the horse is being lazy and not staying on her aids. Unfortunately, until the rider changes her position in the saddle and therefore her biomechanic, there will always be a tug-of-war scenario between the two as the horse is simply responding to his internal laws of balance.

In the third scenario, the rider's upper body has tipped in front of her knee. This means her centre of gravity has moved forwards. In this position, more often than not, the pelvis starts to move into an anterior tilt. This places the seatbones behind the hip joint and at an angle, which causes the front portion of the seat bones to press into the horse's spine. This creates the instant response of the horse hollowing his back away from the pressure; if you have the shape of a hollow back, however you have adjusted your biomechanics to attain

YOUR HIPS CANNOT LIE

If you are suffering from bone degeneration in your hips, or your hips are painful when you ride, it is likely due to your alignment and your footwear. Decades of pushing your pelvis over your knees removes any load to the hips and this can be exacerbated by heeled shoes. Without any load, bones are not motivated to lay down new building blocks to increase their density and strength, so they start to crumble and degenerate. Alignment means that you will encourage new bone growth, creating larger mineral density and strength, and can avoid the pain that comes from a hip that is fraying at the edges.

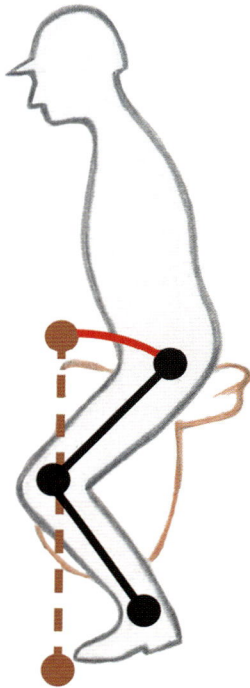

Anterior Tilt
Short arc of rise, horse
will want to rush

This rider has pushed her centre of gravity too far forward, as her pelvis is in an anterior tilt, and she will force the horse to be hollow and quick.

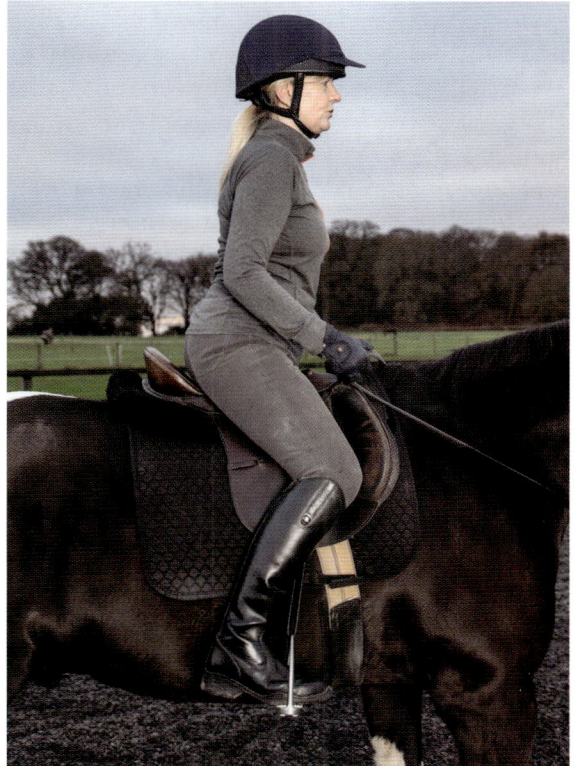

The rider here has a pelvis that is in an anterior tilt, meaning that it is tipping downwards at the front. This increases the curve in the lumbar spine, places the upper body over the knees and reduces the contact the rider has with the saddle. In this position the horse will also have a hollow back.

it, your horse will have a hollow back too, and this is normally accompanied by a raising of his head and neck and his centre of gravity moving backwards.

This rider, having tipped the upper body forwards, now has her centre of gravity slightly in front of the horse's. The arc of the rise is shortened, so the rider's rise will be very shallow and quick. The horse will feel that he needs to move faster to 'catch' the rider, and will speed up to stay in balance. The rider will then feel like she needs to apply rein pressure to slow the horse down, again creating a tug-of-war scenario between the two.

Taking the rider's centre of gravity out of alignment with the horse's centre of gravity in this longitudinal plane means that the horse

will not be able to establish a biomechanically correct way of going. He will not be able to connect along the top line and draw into the contact with his centre of mass moving more underneath the rider.

THE RIBS, TRUNK AND PELVIS

Every move you make (and every move you do not make) affects your pelvis and all the mass it contains. The way structures housed within it absorb load is affected, as already described, by what you wear on your feet, your ankle flexibility and the positioning of your knees. The pelvis enables you to control your horse by shifting weight across the seat bones and the angle it is sitting at. All the pressures of your body positions arrive at your pelvis, and it is of course the way your horse receives the most influential instructions (whether you realize it or not!) It is time now to look above the pelvis at the rib-cage and the muscles of the trunk to find out how they can affect your seat in the saddle. Positional faults occur because the rider is compensating for parts of the body that are weak, parts that are unable to move, parts that are out of alignment and an inability to separate segments of the body.

Many positional weaknesses are shown up through changes of rein, transitions and lateral work. These shifts in direction alter how the horse's base of support needs to be placed to support the change in balance. In these movements the rider's position has the biggest potential to affect how the horse pushes and carries his body, but it also highlights how the rider has been holding their body and how quickly they are able to adjust their own balance to match that of the horse.

SEGMENT CO-DEPENDENCE

Whenever there is a disconnection between the rider's seat and the saddle there are always three things present:

1. a level of immobility through the hips;
2. a co-dependence of movement of the hip, pelvis and lower back; and
3. a weakness of the lower back and therefore poor core proprioception.

These things *always* arise from a lack of alignment and a lack of aligned movement.

LATERAL ASYMMETRIES

Collapsing a hip

A common rider fault is the collapsing of one side of the body, colloquially described as collapsing a hip. This is often a two-fold issue, with a side-bending of the spine one way and a dropping of the hip on the opposite side. This affects both the positioning of the pelvis and the rib-cage in relation to each other and also how the rider's weight is distributed in the saddle. This positional fault has a tendency to be worse on one rein than the other, and in flatwork it is typically highlighted through lateral work, but it can also be seen on straight lines.

Here the rider has collapsed the right hip, leading to asymmetric loading of her weight in the saddle.

The mechanic

Imagine for a moment the rider drops a hip to the right. This means she has collapsed/shortened the space of her waist on the left and her right hip and therefore her right leg is lower than the left. In this position there has been a side-bending of the lumbar spine and a disconnection of alignment between the trunk and the pelvis. More often than not the left seat bone, which has moved slightly to the middle of the saddle, will exert the greatest pressure onto the spine.

The reason for this positional fault (assuming saddle fit is not a problem) is that the rider is unable to separate the movements of the pelvis, hips and lumbar spine, and there is a misinterpretation of sensory/proprioceptive input.

When you change the rein or ask the horse to move laterally, there are a couple of steps that give the horse time to adjust how his limbs are loaded. To help this shift stay in balance the rider has to adjust, very subtly, the weight distribution of her seat. This requires her to move the pelvis very slightly to adjust the weight distribution on the seat bones to align with the new direction of travel. In terms of lateral work, the position of the rider's weight is critical. Balance for the horse in a lateral plane requires him to step underneath and catch the rider's weight. With the rider's centre of gravity a long way from the horse's feet, and with a fairly narrow base of support, the horse is vulnerable to lateral displacement of load. When the rider's weight is distributed via seat bone loading, and the body remains in alignment, the

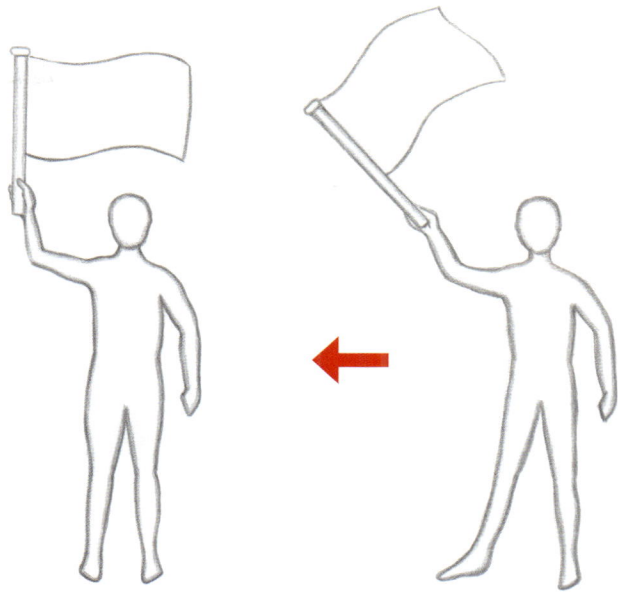

Fig. 32   Flagpole balance. When the balance of something far away from your base of support starts to fall one way, you will step underneath it to catch it. The same is true for your horse. Where your weight goes, he will step underneath to catch you.

horse will move in the direction of the heavier seat bone. His quest is to keep his centre of gravity underneath the rider's, to ensure his position is the most stable. This can be likened to holding a flagpole; if it starts drifting one way you would step underneath it to keep it upright.

The same is true for your horse. If you start leaning your upper body to one side, the horse will step underneath you; the same applies to how you direct weight through your seat bones: your horse will follow the direction of the weight. All lateral asymmetries stem from the co-dependence between parts of the body. This means the body is unable to operate segments individually. You have seen in previous chapters that the hips need to work independently from the pelvis, and the same applies to the pelvis and the lower back. When joints become stuck at the connection point of two different structures, they have to work as a rigid and unyielding mass. Riding requires that you can absorb the movement of the horse, which involves constant adapting, stretching and contracting of muscles and the gentle oscillation of joints. Nothing about sitting in the saddle is static; the rider's body is constantly absorbing, analysing and responding to movement stimuli so when parts cannot be separated to allow the body to adjust positioning in a subtle way, the rider is unable to absorb the horse's movement and begins to affect it in a negative way. It is in this scenario that you will see riders bouncing, tilting their head, gripping or holding on with excess movement of the limbs and/or trunk. More elite riders have developed the systems of reflex throughout their core and joint stabilizers, which allow them to synthesize the movement more intrinsically, without having to recruit the larger, global muscles (or limbs) to stabilize them.

Segment independence of the body is key to a successful seat in the saddle.

LEG POSITION

The role of the legs is both **active** and **passive**. The active role of the rider's leg is to provide motivation to the horse's hind

SEGMENT INDEPENDENCE

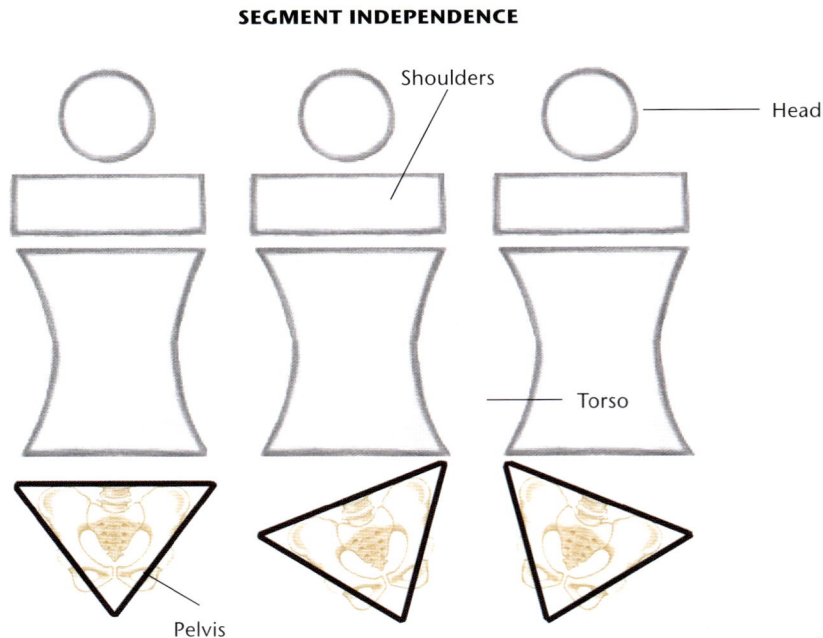

To adjust the weight in the saddle the pelvis needs to change posiiton very slightly. This should not affect the other segments of the body

Fig. 33 Segment independence. The aim of a healthy functioning body is that each segment can move independently. This is especially important in the saddle when the pelvis needs to move but the trunk needs to stay still.

leg to step underneath the body. The calf muscles (below the knee) are responsible for this job, in combination with a soft knee and thigh. The other active role the legs are responsible for is to apply an aid that combines with the seat to slow the forward momentum, balancing the horse's weight onto his hind end. This occurs from the knee and thigh (combined with the rider's seat and back). This use of the legs ensures that the horse is not pulled from the front end to slow down, which shortens the neck, hollows the back and removes engagement of the hind leg.

The more passive role of the legs involves allowing the horse to move forward, lift through the back and have freedom of scapula (shoulder) mobility. This means that the knee and thigh are soft until the horse is required to be more collected and move his centre of gravity backwards. These combinations of roles rely not only on a neutral pelvis but also on a leg that has enough mobility at the hip and enough adductive strength (squeezing towards each other or towards the midline of the body). These attributes can only happen if the relationship between the hips, knees and feet is healthy and aligned. In Chapter 3 the connection of these points was explored, showing how the position of one will affect the others.

The way you are able to use your leg in the saddle will depend on how you load it on the ground, and of course this depends on how the leg is aligned.

RIDING AND HIP POSITION

The very act of sitting in the saddle requires the hips to be moved into external rotation. The width of the horse and the saddle will dictate how much rotation is required. For the hip to be moved in this way, the muscles deep underneath the gluteals and those on the side of the hip have to contract to turn the femur outwards. If, on the ground, your hips face forward and your pelvis and glutes are strong, your hips are likely to have good mobility and this movement is unlikely to cause many issues. However, if you walk with your legs internally or externally rotated, the muscles that are involved with the positioning of the femur are going to be under duress all the time. If the hips internally rotate, these muscles will be stretched, tight and weak, while if the hips are externally rotated, they will be contracted, tight and weak. In addition, the hip joint will be stiff, with tension all around the joint as it will not be sitting squarely in the socket. Asking these muscles to work when you are sitting in the saddle adds further tension to them and the bones will be unable to move to create space and therefore movement ability within the joint. This tension around the joint can create wear and tear and exacerbate problems of hip health.

WALKING PATTERNS

If your feet (or one foot) have collapsed on the inside and your knees are starting to knock inwards, this is over-pronation. In the gait cycle the foot, instead of providing some push, continues to collapse down to the floor. This has ramifications for the entire limb from the foot to the hip and muscle tensions born from this movement cycle will dictate how the limb is able to sit in the saddle, how the limb will interact with the pelvis in the saddle and also how much strength it will have. Feet that turn inwards to face each other are accompanied by an internal rotation of the thigh bone, which positions the knees and hips so that they are also facing inwards. Walking in this way on the ground is incredibly common, and it has far-reaching effects in the saddle. Typically, one foot will tend to over-pronate more than the other, which further complicates how your body is set up to sit in the saddle, as the tensions around your hips, pelvis and into your legs will be different.

Starting from the top, because this is where the problem originates, the deep muscles that are required to pull the hip into external rotation when you sit in the saddle will be stretched and weakened from the constant internal rotation of the femur. Their contractile ability will be poor and the head of the femur itself will be 'stuck' to the socket of the hip joint and unwilling to move. The adductors on the inside of the thigh will be contracted and weak, so leg strength for downward transitions and keeping the horse on your seat will be difficult. In this scenario, when leg pressure is applied, even from the calf, it can pop the rider's seat out of the saddle. This is because the hips are stuck to the pelvis and do not have enough mobility to move slightly in the socket when pressure is applied by the inside of the leg.

Sitting with tight hips disables the ability of the pelvis to really 'plug in' to the saddle, so the rider will be slightly perched in the saddle and unable to use their back or pelvis to really control the position or speed of the horse. Going down the leg, the knees will want to press in towards the saddle flap, blocking the horse's movement of the shoulder. And the problems do not stop at the ankle! A foot that over-pronates will be attached to an ankle that really struggles to interact with the ground, with loads and with communications to the brain. This is because the ligaments will be stretched and weak from the chronic shearing and torque that the bones have to endure as a result of the collapsing foot. As a result, it will try to protect itself from movement so it will become stiff, insensitive and incredibly vulnerable to injury. At foot level, the foot that over-pronates will again not interact with the ground in a way that provides clear proprioceptive feedback, so channels of communication switch off. For riding, the foot and ankle are central segments because of their proprioceptive feedback from being in the stirrups. When this is removed, the body will struggle to find the reaction it must make in order to absorb and coordinate with the horse's movement.

ANKLES

All the joints in the rider's body are required to oscillate when they are in the saddle. This is a small, bouncing action that rises and falls with the horse's trunk as he moves. The greater the speed, or the greater the forces through the body (such as sitting trot, landing after a large jump, canter), the greater the need for the joints to increase their ability to 'bounce'. To create this effect, the bones of the joints require sufficient space to move and they require strong stabilizers to allow them to move. This can only happen if the joints have been moved in a way that allows them to be suspended and decompressed, which can only come from a place of alignment. Ankles that are loaded under shearing or torque conditions, or that have been made immobile through positive heeled shoes, or are attached to feet which do not have any mobility, will be unable to play their critical role in the saddle of flowing with the movement of the horse's body. In terms of positioning in the stirrup, forcing the ankle down creates too much tension in the joint, so it will be unable to absorb any movement. The aim should be to keep the toe and ankle level, and to allow the ankle to have a tiny, imperceptible bounce with the horse's stride.

SITTING TROT

Sitting in the saddle in synchronicity with your horse during sitting trot requires many things to happen. Firstly, your horse's back must be strong enough to cope with the increased amount of loading that occurs when the rider sits for the duration of the stride sequence. In rising trot the rider lifts their body from the horse's back and therefore removes a lot of direct load to the muscles of the back when the horse is pushing his body upwards and forwards (in other words, when the most effort is required). In sitting trot the horse has to create enough force to push his body up and forwards whilst carrying the rider on his back muscles. The horse will only have a strong enough back if he has been worked in a way that supports this strengthening.

When the horse's back is lifted and he is pushing evenly with both hind legs (travelling straight through his body) and is drawing into an even contact with a soft neck, the muscles of the back can act as a trampoline for the rider. If the horse is worked with a braced neck and a braced back that is hollow, he is crooked and working with muscles in tension not tone, the back will behave like a springboard, sending all the energy back up into the rider's body in a ricochet type of feeling. This contributes to the bouncing or instability in the saddle that many riders experience during sitting trot. In essence, if a horse is moving in this way, his back is not strong or conditioned enough to be expected to move well with a rider in sitting trot.

The rider also plays a significant role, not just in the way they are training the horse, but in the shape, alignment, mobility and strength of their body. The mechanic of sitting trot requires the rider's body to absorb forces from the horse's body moving upwards, downwards, forwards and side to side. As the trot is a diagonal, two-beat pace it activates the diagonal postural slings in both horse and rider. The symmetry of tone in these slings is especially important when the rider is required to absorb the loads the horse is creating with every step. This connects directly to how straight the horse is; is he pushing evenly from both hind legs and therefore sending equal amounts of tension through the rider's pelvis? And is the rider sitting evenly or is there too much tension on one side which blocks the horse from stepping through evenly?

In order for horse and rider to stay connected and synchronized in sitting trot, the rider's body has to do three things:

1. the hips have to move independently from the pelvis;
2. the pelvis has to move independently from the lower back; and
3. the muscles of the lower back have to be strong to direct the right reflex through to the rest of the core to maintain the rider's balance.

CANTER

The same principles of segment independence also apply in the canter. The rider's pelvis needs to stay in contact with the saddle so that the aids for direction and engagement can be transmitted. If the pelvis cannot move independently to move with the horse's canter stride and therefore absorb the forces of the stride through its movement and transference to the core, the seat will bounce up and down and the body will be incredibly rigid, or the upper body will try to offset the bounce by swinging backwards and forwards like a pendulum.

When the pelvis and hips are independent of each other, and of the rest of the body, they will allow movement and force absorption, which means the rest of the body can stay still. To sit in balance in the canter, imagine that you have separated your core from your pelvis. You want your pelvis to stay connected to the saddle, but you want to lift or hold your upper body slightly distant from it. This helps to create the feeling of segment independence and can be really useful in learning how to absorb movement through the lower half of your body.

THE UPPER BODY

How's your contact?

Don't panic all at once! Contact can be the topic that wakes you up in a cold sweat at 3am; you have too much, you don't have enough, is it elastic? How do you make it elastic? What does that even mean? Your arms ache and your knuckles turn white. Echoes of 'keep your hands *still*' shudder through your body as your instructor's voice revisits you in the small hours. Overly dramatic? Maybe. But achieving the contact of your (and your horse's) dreams can be an agonizing process.

When we talk about contact we are referring to the communication of your aids through your reins. To analyse what constitutes a 'good' contact could, and probably would, take us far away from the context of this book. However, there are several aspects to contact that you should be thinking about:

- Are your communications through the reins as clear as possible? (How much white noise are you creating, or how much are you restricting?)
- How consistent are you? (What part are you playing in the state of your contact?)
- Do YOU influence the contact, or does your horse? Who has more of a say in what you feel in your hands?

The complexity of contact means that the state of it involves a wide array of factors, but it is also the state of it that determines and tells the biggest story about how your horse is moving, and how you are sitting in the saddle. It is the melting point of problems elsewhere in the horse's body (in terms of training). For example, a hind leg that is not carrying load or pushing load sufficiently will be felt in the contact, as will a disconnection across the top line or an overloading of the forehand.

The way you as a rider sit and influence the contact comes first from how you are able to use your body, and secondly from the misty murky waters of 'feel'.

Hands, arms, elbows, shoulders, back

Communication through the reins with your hands is at the end of the communication channel; it is not the beginning. Your hands are attached to your arms, which are attached to your shoulders, which are attached to your shoulder blades, which are attached to your thoracic spine (*see* Chapter 2).

Isolating the hands to correct a contact issue would be as illogical as trying to fix the wheel alignment in your car by looking only at the steering wheel. It might be the thing that starts juddering at 40mph but the problem is in the tyres, which are connected to the drive shaft, which attaches to the steering wheel. The steering wheel is the last point in the line of trouble, not the cause of the trouble.

Unsteady hands or hands that create too much restriction are a symptom of an issue elsewhere. The health of the hands on a micro level (tension of soft tissues) may contribute to the overall tension in the forearm, and therefore into the shoulder, but it is more likely that the problems have begun with the connection of the arms to the body. Once again, we need to look at how we are using our bodies most of the time.

Your arms, shoulders and hands would, at one point along the evolutionary trail, have been used in making things, carrying things, pulling things towards the body and pushing things away from the body. They would have spent most of the day in various positions, using varying amounts of strength to manage loads in a variety of different ways. The continual innervation created by use ensured that the anchor of the arms (where the shoulder blades attach to the spine) was strong and stable.

The chances are you now use your arms for fewer things, and more of those things will involve resting on a keypad or some repetitive movement that uses the arms without the need for a strong anchored point. When you come to ride and strive to create a consistent,

elastic feel in the reins, loading the hands and/or asking the arms to stay still becomes unachievable if your arms do not have a strong attachment to the body, your shoulders are stiff and immobile and there is tension through the top of the body and into the neck. If the upper body is out of alignment with the hips and the muscular attachments of the shoulder girdle are weak, you will instead hold the reins with tension, creating a contact that is brittle as opposed to elastic.

Riding requires that the arms are loaded with a bent elbow. This is not the same loading pattern that you would experience when you carry a bucket of water with straight arms and the load hanging from the bottom. This creates a drag on the shoulder joint and the muscles of the neck and top of shoulders, but

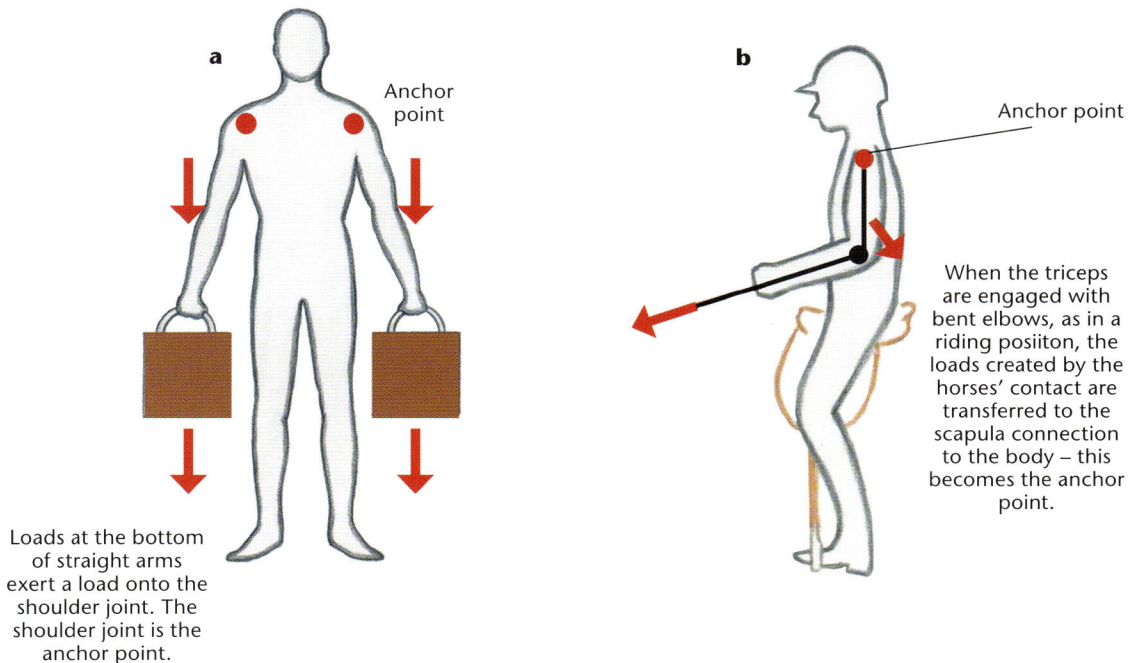

a

Anchor
point

Loads at the bottom
of straight arms
exert a load onto the
shoulder joint. The
shoulder joint is the
anchor point.

b

Anchor point

When the triceps
are engaged with
bent elbows, as in a
riding posiiton, the
loads created by the
horses' contact are
transferred to the
scapula connection
to the body – this
becomes the anchor
point.

Fig. 34   Loading the arms.
a) Loading straight arms creates a pull onto the shoulder joints as these are the anchor points.
b) Arms with bent elbows have the shoulder girdle as the anchor point; in this case the load is directed to the
*   back of the body. This is why a strong shoulder girdle is so important for a good contact.*

with the arms in the same plane as the body the attachment of the arms to the body via the scapula is not supremely tested. With a bent elbow, the drag and therefore load of the neck and shoulder muscles is transferred to the back of the body. With the arms in a horizontal plane, loading the hands has the potential to pull the body off balance, so the anchor point of the scapula is essential.

Regular arm movements off-horse, as you have seen, create a stable foundation for the arms to move and to be loaded from various positions, and in order to be elastic or have any form of controlled or intentional movement, things must first be stable.

Upper body positioning, and therefore the positioning of the scapula relative to the thoracic spine, is largely dependent upon the position of the pelvis. It is not possible to have a consistent, elastic contact if the upper body is not in alignment with the hips. If the ribs are pushed forwards and upwards creating a shearing position of the thoracic vertebrae, the muscles that attach to the scapula do not have an aligned position to work from. The lines of pull are contorted. If you come to the saddle as an habitual hip thruster, with a pelvis out of neutral, your thoracic spine will be immobile, your arms will have a weak connection and your contact will reflect this.

BENDING THE ELBOWS

Imagine for a moment you are holding the reins. Your elbows should be bent and by your sides. Loading the hands at the end of bent arms is different from loading the hands at the end of straight arms. When you carry something heavy from a straight arm you apply load and 'drag' to your shoulder joint. When you have load in your hands with a bent elbow, the load is directed to the shoulder girdle, and more

specifically the scapula. It can be useful to make your elbows 'heavy' by pressing down to the ground with them. This activates the muscles that will help to stabilize the scapula, improving the connection to the torso and enabling you to have a more elastic contact without being tense through the forearms.

A NOTE ON TRAINING

The state of your contact is also connected to the way you train, and the stage of training your horse has reached. The aim as a rider is to be the influencer of the contact, rather than have your contact be influenced by the horse.

The horse will only ever feel even and elastic on the end of the reins if he is moving straight and drawing over the topline. A horse that moves crookedly is pushing unevenly from his hind legs, which means he will load his shoulders unevenly, which means he will load the bit unevenly. Where the horse's centre of gravity is (and therefore where yours is) will also affect how he is able to load the bit. We have seen how your position in rising trot will affect the positioning of the horse's head and neck, and these positions will absolutely affect how you and your horse are able to meet from your hands to his mouth. How the horse accepts the bit can be influenced as well by teeth, bit and bridle, or pain somewhere in the body. The state of your contact is an amalgamation of how you are influencing the horse's body, how reactive he is to your aids, how you are sitting and whether or not one or both of you are in pain. The rider's responsibility is absolute. You are responsible for how you are training the horse, and you are responsible for creating an environment where the horse is encouraged into your hand. Hands which hold on, restrict or pull will be met with equal or greater resistance from the horse, and hands that cannot hold and adjust to the positioning and idiosyncrasies of how a horse comes to the bit and into the hand will not be able to create somewhere for the horse to land.

In both scenarios the horse is unable to be worked fully through the body in a way that is biomechanically sound. From a training perspective, the aim is always to achieve a true connection of the horse's body from the hind legs through into the contact. Only when this is attained can the horse move comfortably, in a way that suits his biomechanical make-up. In order to connect the hind end to the front, the horse must be straight, as then he is loading each side of his body and dealing with the load evenly. He is then able to transmit the same amount of load through the body into the forelimbs and therefore into the contact. The other essential component of connection is the environment you as a rider provide for the horse to connect into. If you consider the top line of the horse as an elastic band, then in order to put energy into that band it needs to be anchored at both ends. The same is true if you are going to create energy from the hind end and move it through the horse's body. It needs to have load at both ends. The hind leg push is load from the back, and feeling the horse come into the contact is load at the front. For this reason it is your job as a rider to keep the contact straight and consistent (as in feel the horse's mouth) so the horse has a landing beacon to reach for.

FEEL

You have probably been exposed to the concept of 'feel' as it relates to riding. It is the attribute which turns elite riders into horse whisperers but which leaves the rest floundering and searching for the holy grail.

What feel really means is the ability to have a subtle and well-timed ability to make an adjustment to the signal you are sending the horse. For some people, this comes quite naturally; there is an intuitive element that allows them to adjust without much conscious thought. For the rest of the riding population, it does not come so easily.

Firstly, in order to make subtle adjustments in load, pressure and the direction of these, there must be control over the arms and a stable anchor (as we have seen). The second part, the timing, largely comes from an intuitive place, but often body awareness, highly attuned proprioceptive programming and practice can improve the rider's ability to 'feel' when an adjustment needs to be made. And yes, you've guessed it, this is all improved if the body is moved frequently, differently and with mindfulness.

STABILIZERS VS MOVERS

Joints are stabilized by the small muscles that lie closest to them. These muscles are responsible for maintaining the integrity of the joint whilst it is being asked to move. When these muscles (and ligaments) are strong, it frees up the larger, more global muscles to ask for the movement and not to worry about having to stay in tension to help provide support to the joints. If you suffer with too much tension in your body when you ride, you may well be relying on your movement muscles to do more of the stabilizing work than they should be. It is essential that in absorbing the movement from the horse the joints use their own network of support staff, and do not borrow from the movement team. There is such a huge amount of sensory input to your body that the large, movement muscles need to be available to absorb it and deal with it. If they are desperately trying to keep your back safe, for example, they will not have the suppleness they need to soak up all the loads the horse provides. If they are held in a tense state it creates a level of rigidity throughout your body and the loads are taken into the body as concussion rather than bounce. This creates excess movement and instability in the saddle, which will encourage the horse to hollow and brace his back. The same principles apply to your horse's body. The muscles of the lumbar region should be bouncy to touch. When the vertebral stabilizers have been switched off through incorrect training/poor movement, then the global, superficial muscles will brace to support the back. This creates a rigidity of movement which will be difficult for the rider to sit on.

Part 2

The Pillars of Your Future Movement Story

In Part 1, you learnt how your body is designed to be used and how, through culture and movement environments, these inbuilt movement protocols have been largely 'lost in translation'. This lack of knowledge about how the body can be used in a way that strengthens it and protects against pain and injury is leaving people with constant pain, dysfunction and a body shape that is confusing as well as frustrating. As a rider, your body is your biggest tool, and trying to get it into the right position with the right amount of strength and coordination is a journey you are willing to take, but progress seems a little too slow. As research into horse and rider performance becomes increasingly insightful, the effect the rider has on the way the horse moves and his subsequent soundness has become a fact that no one can hide from. What you do in the saddle affects your horse.

The aim of this book is to give you an understanding of the fundamental movement principles that still reside within your body and how to use them to your advantage. All too often symptoms are treated whilst the cause is overlooked, and this is certainly the case when it comes to ailments of your physical body. Unless attributable to a recent physical trauma, the symptoms you experience – whether it comes in the form of sciatica, hip pain, knee pain or back pain – arise because of the way you are loading your body, and the way you are loading your body is dictated by the position you move it in. To conquer the symptoms, the body needs to be moved differently.

In Part 2 you will be taken through the four pillars of movement training that will start the transformation of your body as soon as you begin. To change anything we are used to takes time, and this is especially true in the mobilizing and strengthening sections. The first two pillars, however, can be implemented immediately, and your body will begin to benefit from them as soon as you start.

The four pillars of movement health are:

- Alignment
- Expansion
- Mobilizing
- Strengthening

5 Alignment

Chapter 2 explored the importance of having the body in an aligned posture. Alignment matters for joints to be able to move through their full range of movement, for muscles to build their optimal strength, for the lower back to be decompressed and stable, and for the correct function of the entire breathing apparatus. Knowing how to move your body from a place of alignment is the fundamental, most critical step for initiating positive change in how your body is going to look, feel and function in the saddle. The beauty about alignment is that you can make the changes immediately. By altering how you position your body, you will immediately apply different loads to different areas. This might mean that you remove damaging loads to some joints and start firing up essential muscles that may have been asleep.

The recurring theme through the first half of the book has been load and how it impacts your body. The way your body is organized determines how the loads it experiences are going to sculpt it and whether it is going to be strengthened or weakened, mobilized or stiffened, functional or dysfunctional. If you take a class, or have guidance from someone at the gym, you are probably advised how to adopt the correct 'form' for the exercise you are about to do. It is actually the same when you have a lesson on your horse; your instructor will advise you, and try to manoeuvre you into the correct 'form' for sitting in the saddle in the best way for the discipline you have chosen. As you saw in the beginning section of the book, the form

you have your body in for a few hours a week does not offset the form your body is in all the time. The body you take to class is still full of muscle imbalances, joint stiffness and postural deviations. It doesn't immediately become functional and able to cope with loads to new areas, and quite often you will not be able to get it into the correct form that might help prevent injury anyway. The answer is to improve how the body is arranged so that the loads it experiences can be handled in a way that improves the state of your musculo-skeletal system. Your body will deal with the same loads whether it is aligned or not; the difference lies in the impact the loads will have.

As a rider, your body has to deal with more loads, geometry and sensory input than a non-riding human, and if you move out of alignment on the ground your body is pulled into a shape that does not lend itself to being in the right position when you ride; the geometry of a comfortable and balanced riding position is not possible if the body has been pulled in all directions, yet hours are spent trying to correct the position in the saddle. To ask the body to be in a different shape when it is on an unstable surface and faced with a whole new set of loads should suddenly appear fairly illogical.

Riders come in all shapes and sizes, and each body will receive and respond to the loads it experiences from the horse in a slightly different way. This is down to natural biology (length of bones, for example) and the health of the tissues, which is determined by how the body is moved every day. The great news is that whatever shape your body is currently in, it is possible to improve its alignment right now.

The following photos show various riders all with a different posture that is 'normal' for them. None of these postures is natural for the body and all of them are out of alignment, but they feel normal and comfortable to the people who have adopted them. You might be able to identify with some of these shapes, and it is likely that one of them will be the shape you have been moving in for a number of years. These postures can all create muscular tensions, inappropriate loads on joints and a body that is vulnerable to injury.

YOUR STANDING AND WALKING ALIGNMENT HOW-TO

Aligning your body is similar to stacking building blocks. The aim is to put the bones into vertical alignment so they can resist gravity, maintain joint space and keep the correct curvature of the spine. By getting the body into a position where these things are enabled, the cascade effect of improved muscular activity helps to strengthen and therefore maintain this alignment so that it can become more of a movement habit.

There are five steps to alignment:

1. **Feet.** When standing, always stand with your feet facing straight ahead and hip

a), b), c) Examples of postures that are out of alignment, but that feel very normal and are adopted most of the time.

a), b), c) Postures that have been aligned by backing the hips over the heels, dropping the ribs over the pelvis, the shoulders over the ribs and the chin back towards the neck.

width apart. Standing with your feet together places too much torque onto the hip joint. By keeping your feet hip width apart, you make sure that your thigh bone is sitting vertically, helping the hip to maintain space within the socket.

2. **Pelvis/Hips/Heels.** Move your hips back so they are sitting over your heels. This might seem like a long way back, and you might feel slightly unbalanced. If so, that's just because your glutes have not been working as much as they should and are not used to holding you up. The chances are you have been loading the quads at the front of your body and

loading your knees; if you have knee pain/hip pain/lower back pain/foot pain and/or pelvic floor trouble, it is highly likely that your pelvis has been sitting over your knees not your heels. As you saw in Chapter 2, the hips are the largest joint in the body and are designed to take the most load. Your heel is designed to deal with the initial impact of hitting the ground, and then to dissipate this force throughout the foot and up the leg. The front of the foot is not designed to be overloaded as its role is to be dextrous and mobile. By moving your pelvis and therefore your hips over your heels you have immediately changed how your body is going to deal with load. It is a posture that strengthens the hip joints, glutes and hamstrings, and with good heel strike on the ground it helps to build bone density.

3. **Ribs.** As you have seen, rib thrust causes havoc with vertebral alignment and therefore health. Thrusting the ribs creates a step effect within the thoracic vertebrae, which are then incredibly vulnerable to any twisting movements of the torso and any loads that are applied to the arms. Thrusting the ribs also creates a hollow and therefore compressed posture of the lower back, disabling the muscles from activating and therefore strengthening from any movements you might do. To correct their positioning you need to drop the bottom rib so that it is sitting in a vertical line with your pelvis.

4. **Shoulders.** Moving your shoulders into the right position may feel odd and a bit 'slumped' at first, as it is very common for people to continuously try to pull their shoulders back to improve their posture. This goes back to the illusion that bringing the shoulders back is a corrective movement; as you now know, it does not change the curvature of your thoracic spine – the area that is causing your shoulders to appear in a poor posture. To start to activate and strengthen the muscles of the shoulder and upper back where the arms are connected to the body, you need to let the shoulders settle over your ribs. In this position it might be easier to see the increased curve at the top of your spine; this is the shape of your body and the fix is shown on the next page, but it has nothing to do with pulling your shoulders back!

5. **Chin.** The chin has a sneaky habit of moving away from the body, and this adds a massive weight to the top of your spine, which requires an excess of muscular tension to support. This is a massive contributor to headaches, and neck and shoulder tension. To remedy the problem, bring the chin back towards the body by lifting the base of your skull upwards. This should create a few chins (the more the merrier!). Try this when you are driving and when you are sitting at your desk. Leaning forward towards a screen is a hotspot for this misalignment to creep in.

Through making these adjustments, you can change how your body deals with load straightaway, and you will have started your journey to a stronger, less painful and more functional body.

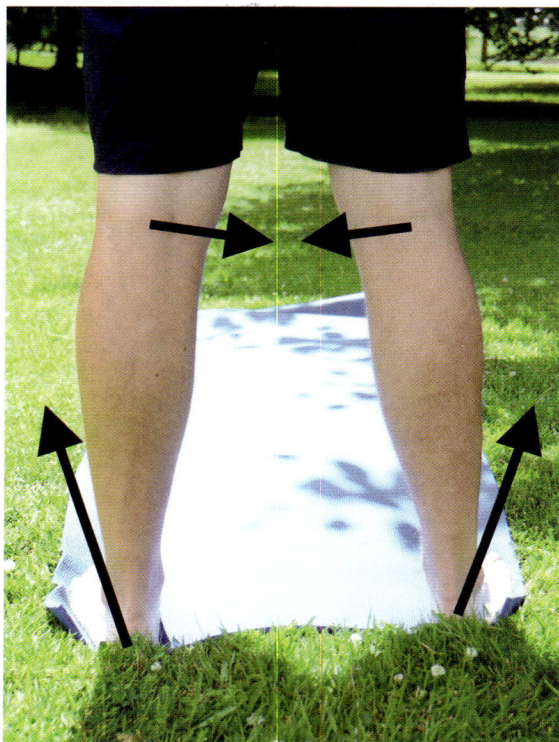

Feet that sit in an over-pronated position are very common. This creates torque to the knees and the hips.

FEET AND KNEES

The five steps listed above are the foundation for standing and walking alignment, but adjustments may not stop there if you typically walk with your knees crashing into each other. If you have habitually walked with your leg bones rotating inwards, simply straightening your feet will not stack the bones correctly, and will displace the loads to a different side of your knees and hips.

The problem with rotation, over-pronation and any general misalignment of your bones is that the bones receive load on the edge of their surface, rather than squarely. Like the tyres on a car, which will wear unevenly if the steering alignment is out of kilter, so too will your joints. The aim should always be to load the joints as squarely as possible so that load can be distributed over as large an area as possible. This loading pattern on the edge of joints is shown up in the form of bunions on the feet, and joint degeneration of the knees and hips.

Once you have faced your feet forward, you need to make sure that the knee creases at the back of your knee are sitting centrally rather than off to one side. To get them to be central, you may need to rotate your femurs outwards.

It is likely that this is going to feel a bit strange, so initially aim to make these adjustments when you are standing and be mindful of how you are placing your feet and knees when you walk. Remember that transformation occurs drip by drip; small adjustments that you can do as often as possible will reap the biggest rewards.

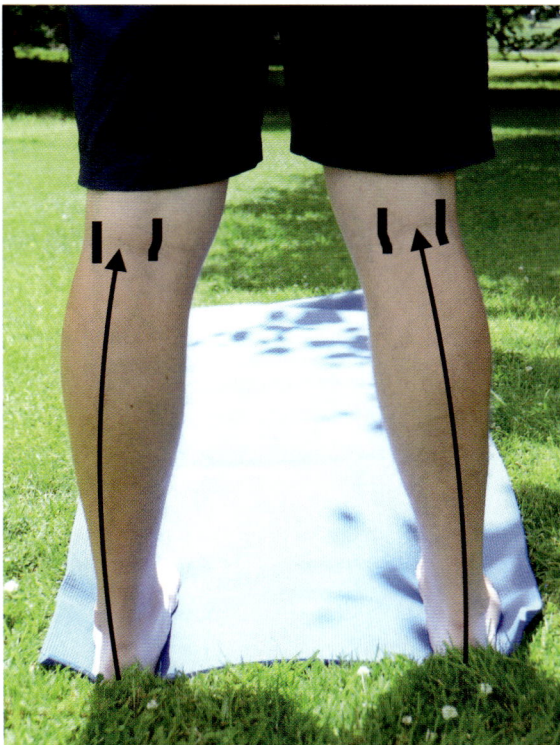

Although the feet have been straightened, the knees are still off-centre because the femur has not been straightened.

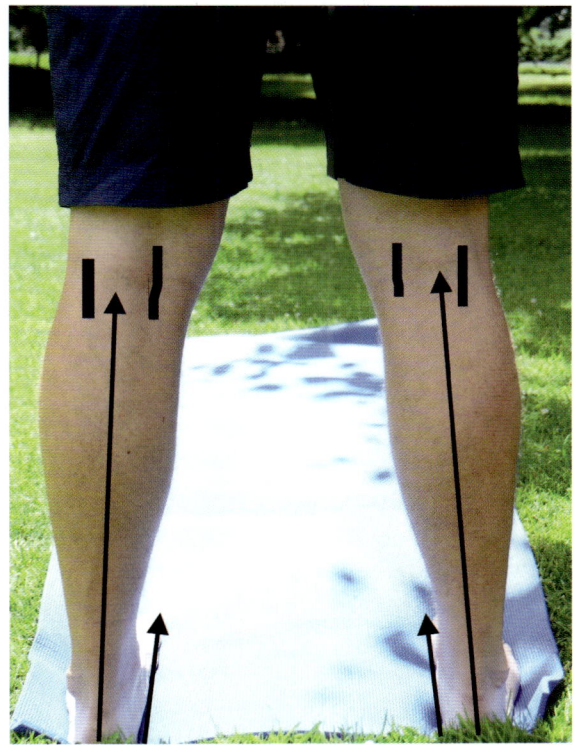

Correcting the alignment of the femur means that now the knee creases are finally at centre.

WALKING IN ALIGNMENT

a) and b) Walking in alignment means that you maintain the shoulder, hip and heel positioning both on the flat, and up and down hills. This builds strength in the back of your body, strengthens the hips and protects the knees from too much load.

SITTING ALIGNMENT

You have read about the impact too much sitting can have on your body, but the reality is that sitting is now a big part of life that would be reasonably impractical to remove, so the aim has to be to minimize its effects as much as possible. This includes taking regular walk breaks. In the next few chapters you will learn some movements that you can do to unravel some of the tensions that

sitting can create. In terms of alignment, you can make sitting less impactful on the body if you aim to keep the same rules of alignment.

Always have your feet flat on the floor and try to avoid crossing your legs, which is easier said than done! The pelvis, as the base of support in the chair, often becomes tucked underneath and you end up sitting on your sacrum. This has consequences for the health of your pelvic

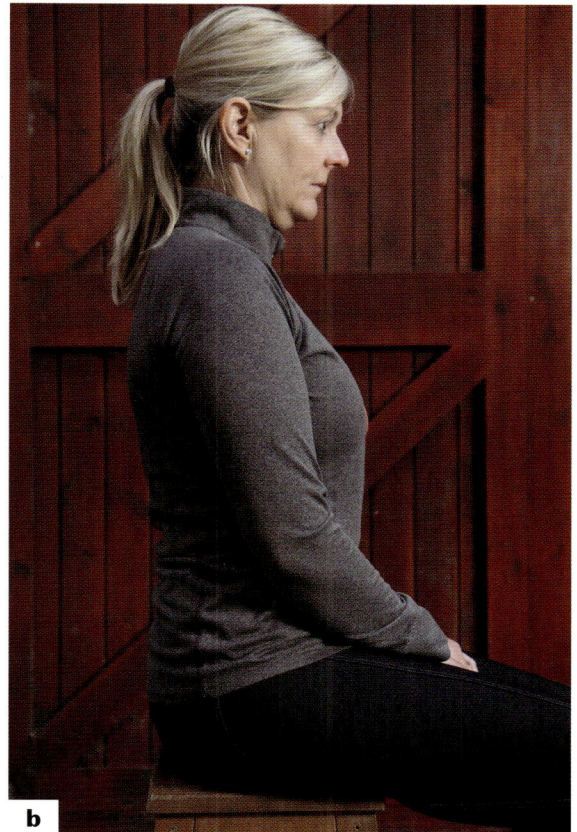

Sitting creates a lot of problems for the body. a) The lower back flexes, the shoulders move in front of the hips and the chin moves away from the spine. This creates detrimental loading to the neck and the entire spinal column. b) Aim to sit in alignment by keeping the pelvis in neutral, and the shoulders over the hips. Keep pulling your chin towards the neck during the day

floor muscles, as well as your lower back, as it encourages it into a flexed position. The foundation for alignment in the chair is to keep the pelvis in neutral, so you are loading your seat bones rather than the sacrum. Next you need to drop your ribs so they are over the top of your pelvis, and then line up your shoulders with your ribs. Your chin is likely to creep forward during the day, so set a reminder or try to build a habit that checks in with your chin position so that you can draw it back towards the body to keep the neck and top of the back happy.

LYING ALIGNMENT

In Chapter 3 you learnt about rib thrust, and it has cropped up frequently throughout the book in terms of how damaging and vulnerable it can make the spine. The problem with constantly thrusting your ribs is that it becomes a posture that is constantly with you; the tissues get cast into this position, so even when you lie down it is still there. This is not so much of a problem when you lie down to sleep, but if you are at a class and have to do some form of exercise whilst lying on your back, your rib thrusting habit

Rib thrust creates problems for the spine when you do exercises lying down. Bolster the space beneath your ribs to bring them back into alignment.

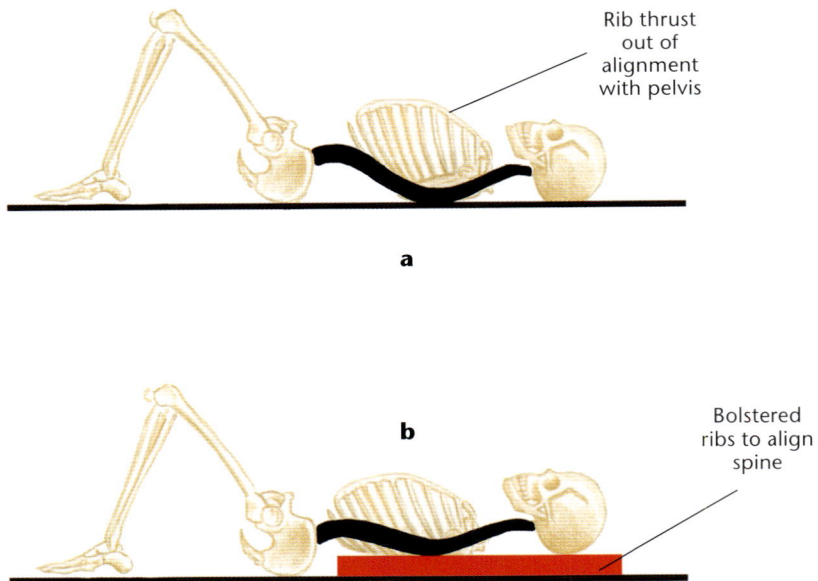

Rib thrust out of alignment with pelvis

a

Bolstered ribs to align spine

b

Fig. 35 Lying alignment.
a) Rib thrust creates a misalignment of the spine when you lie down. The ribs need to be dropped to be in line with the pelvis to be safe to add any load or movement to the spine.
b) Fill the space underneath your thrusted ribs with a bolster or rolled-up towel to bring the spine back into alignment.

can leave your spine open to loads that it cannot cope with. The answer is to support the spine by aligning it within this rib thrust until you have moved the ribs back into place through daily strengthening and mobilizing movements.

Lie on your back; if you find there is a lot of space underneath the middle of your back through to your pelvis, the chances are your ribs are being thrust. To support the spine in this position, you need to bolster the ribs until the length of the spine aligns. In other words, you need to artificially fill the gap your rib thrust has created. You can use a bolster or a rolled up towel or cushions to give you this support. This can be shown in the following diagram and photos.

Aligning your body is one of the best things you can do for it, and it is something you can implement straight away. By securing the shoulder, hip, heel alignment on the ground you will find it a lot easier to maintain the same positional guidelines in the saddle. It will help strengthen the entire posterior chain, which enables your core to switch on and it ensures that your hips stay as mobile as possible, which is essential if they are going to survive without wearing out after hours and hours sitting in a saddle.

6 Expansion Breathing

Thankfully, remembering to breathe does not have to be on your daily 'to do' list. You do not have to fit it in around other chores; in fact you do not *have* to give it any conscious thought at all. As you continue to read, you might become aware of how oxygen is coming into your body, and the gentle rise and fall of your rib-cage, and as you settle in you might relax your abdomen and start to take deeper breaths.

Breathing is incredibly powerful; not only does it keep you alive, it also serves you on a mechanical and neurological level as well. This chapter explores the brilliance of breathing, and how it can impact your riding.

THE PHYSIOLOGY OF BREATHING

Breathing brings life-giving oxygen (O_2) into the body and removes toxic carbon dioxide (CO_2), a waste product of respiration. Your breathing is controlled by the autonomic nervous system, which is what enables it to happen without you thinking about it. The brainstem houses respiratory nerve centres which automatically send signals to the diaphragm and intercostals to contract and relax in a steady rhythm, keeping the balance of oxygen and carbon dioxide at a healthy level. Throughout the circulatory system, oxygen and carbon dioxide receptors monitor the levels of each gas present in the blood. When the amount of oxygen decreases (relative to the amount of carbon dioxide) the respective informants will send a signal to the brainstem that a breath needs to occur. This is why, when you hold your breath, you are forced to release it and inhale, because the concentration of carbon dioxide becomes too high and potentially hazardous to your body.

When you move with greater intensity – walking uphill, running or riding – your muscles require more oxygen to provide them with nutrients and energy to keep working. This means the usage of oxygen and the build-up of waste happens much more quickly, so the speed of your breathing increases.

Most of the time you breathe using the upper portion of your chest and the upper portion of your lungs. It is rare to take a deep breath and fill the lungs in their entirety. This shallow breathing, although common, has consequences for how your body can function, and how your nervous system behaves.

THE MECHANICS OF BREATHING

Although it is very useful to have such a critical, life-sustaining action taken care of for you, not thinking about how you breathe, or not doing activities that force the mechanic to occur as it really should, means that you are missing out on a whole host of improvements to your body that can happen just through breathing more efficiently.

When your body is engaged in physical activity, your lungs are designed to fully inflate to take in as much oxygen as possible to nourish muscles that are working harder than they do at rest. Evolution was pretty cunning and made sure that this expansion provided support and stability to the trunk so that during physical activity the limbs could move independently from a strong base. Expanding the rib-cage also provides traction and support to the thoracic spine, giving the centre of the body stability. The diaphragm at the top of the core is activated, drawing down and increasing the pressure within the chest cavity. Through being switched on, it provides strength to the top of the core cylinder so that this muscular section of the body can be strong, too.

THE SKELETON AND BREATHING

The skeleton is only able to do everything it is capable of if the lungs are inflated to capacity.

BREATHING IN (INHALATION)

The purpose with every inhalation is for the body to receive as much oxygen as possible. For this to happen, the rib-cage needs to expand by lifting up and out on all sides of the cage (front, sides and back) to allow the lungs to inflate.

One of the most basic processes in the body is the function of the diaphragm (the large sheet of muscle that separates the chest from the abdomen, sitting below the rib-cage). As you saw in Chapter 2, it creates the top of the core. In a resting position, the diaphragm sits in a shallow dome shape. To allow air into the lungs the diaphragm contracts, which flattens it, allowing space for the lungs to draw down into as they expand. The rib-cage should be lifted as high and wide as possible to allow the lungs maximum space to inflate inside this protective cage. As the ribs attach to the thoracic vertebrae, this expansion also provides

essential traction to the vertebrae, helping to stabilize the spine.

When the body is in full inhalation, with fully inflated lungs, the torso is at its strongest and all the tissues are receiving the oxygen they need to keep functioning. When the spine is well supported due to the increase of intervertebral space and muscular recruitment, the appendicular skeleton (limbs) can operate independently. The aim should be that this posture is maintained for as long as possible, which means the torso is kept in expansion for as much of the exhalation process as possible.

When breathing in happens only in the top half of your chest and you never fully fill your lungs, you recruit the muscles of the chest and neck to bring a small amount of air in. This creates tension in the neck and contracts the muscles of the chest, which impacts how the shoulders can move, and how mobile and comfortable your neck will be. It also means that the potential benefit of full lung breathing is never realized.

Very often riders will forget about the importance of their breathing when they are nervous, anxious or concentrating. The problem with this is that holding your breath stimulates more of a fear response in the body, and in Chinese medicine this tension is said to be held in the lower back. By introducing some expansion breaths as a new habit at the beginning of and during your ride, you can begin to bring this essential process to the saddle in a way that is going to benefit your performance.

BREATHING OUT (EXHALATION)

Normally, the breathing out process requires no effort at all. As the time comes for air to leave the lungs, so the diaphragm relaxes, returning to its dome shape. This helps to push air out of the lungs, which then start to collapse, creating enough space for the next in-breath. However, as we know, the diaphragm is the top of the core and it is controlled by muscles, so bringing some strength to this area by holding the ribs in expansion benefits the entire cylinder of the core. To do this means that the position of the diaphragm needs to be controlled. If you can direct the speed at which the diaphragm returns to its resting position, you can control how air leaves your lungs, how much of it leaves your lungs and for how long your spine and limbs are going to feel stable and supported. To do this, you need to control how much air leaves your lungs at any one time. You want to release it in increments, a bit like blowing through a narrow straw, without drawing your tummy button in towards your spine. This action recruits the entire core group, lengthens the spine and strengthens the muscles of the diaphragm, so that when you are in the saddle you will have the strength to control how you are breathing in any situation.

THE NEUROLOGICAL RESPONSE TO BREATHING

Your body's levels of stress hormones are controlled by the autonomic nervous system (the same one that tells your body when to breathe). This system has two components: the sympathetic nervous system, which gets the body ready for action and floods it with stress hormones and adrenaline, and its counterpart the parasympathetic nervous system, which works to calm you down, lowers your heart rate and blood pressure and improves digestion and the uptake of nutrients. The interesting point is that the very action of breathing taps into this calming system via a major nerve (the Vagus nerve), which runs

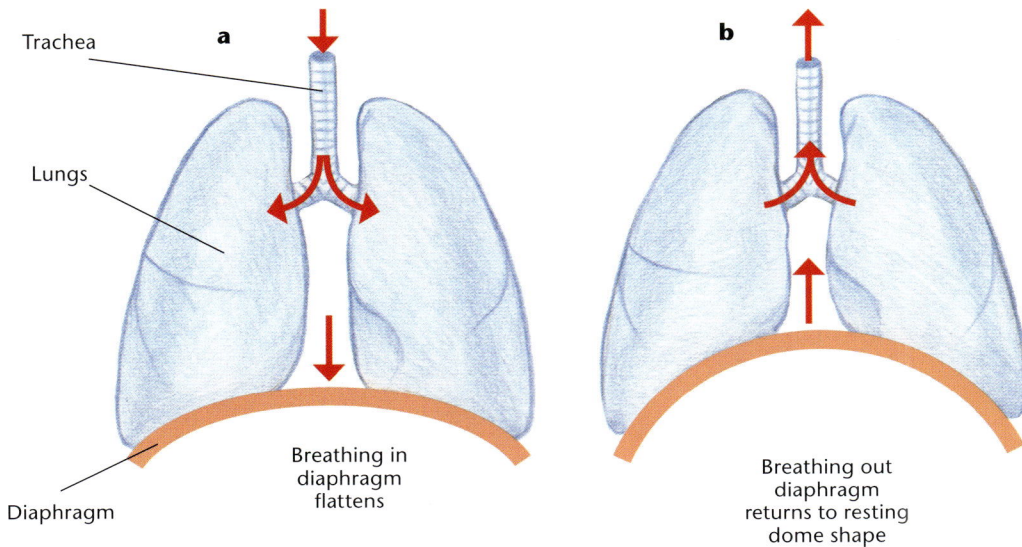

Trachea

Lungs

Diaphragm

a Breathing in diaphragm flattens

b Breathing out diaphragm returns to resting dome shape

Fig. 36   The mechanics of breathing.
a)   The diaphragm flattens during inhalation to allow the lungs space to expand into.
b)   The diaphragm returns to a resting dome shape during exhalation. The upward curve helps to push air out of the lungs.

through the diaphragm. When the diaphragm contracts, the parasympathetic nervous system kicks in. By keeping the diaphragm engaged for as long as possible during the breathing cycle, you are able to reduce the stress hormones in your body, as well as improve it on a mechanical level.

IMPACT FOR RIDERS

BREATHE BETTER, LIVE BETTER

Impeded breathing short-changes everything. It disrupts the functions of the organs, slows metabolism, creates chronic pain and upsets digestion.

Breathing out correctly is also crucial to you as a rider. Some trainers encourage you to breathe out for downward transitions, so that you can increase your horse's connection. Why? Once you can control your exhalation you should feel why; you are now holding your own weight within your body, the pressures created through controlled exhalation help to stabilize the torso, the expansion of your ribs keeps your spine open and tall and you have removed tension from the muscles of your lower back.

The benefits of good breathing for riding

- It lowers the heart rate for you and your horse
- By exhaling correctly you recruit trunk-stabilizing muscles, which will help control downward transitions

- Muscles can work longer and more effectively with better oxygen supply
- Expanding the rib-cage to inhale improves upper body posture, the connection of spine, pelvis and hips and the strength of the shoulder girdle
- Correct breathing maintains a long and strong torso which is essential for balance, independent aids and synchronicity with your horse

TECHNIQUE

Stand with your feet hip width apart in neutral spine and with the back of the head lifted. Rock your weight back over your heels, and have a very small bend in the knee ('soft knees'). Place your little finger on the top of your pelvis and your thumb touching your bottom rib.

Place your little finger on the top of your pelvis and your thumb underneath your bottom rib.

Lift and expand the rib-cage so you increase the space between your thumb and little finger. Hold this expansion for as long as possible.

To INHALE: take a deep breath in and increase the space between your thumb and little finger. The rib-cage should rise as the diaphragm flattens to allow the lungs to expand and to draw air in. Your shoulders shouldn't move; all the movement should come from the ribs. Imagine that you are filling the lower back lobes of your lungs. Try to breathe in for a count of five.

To EXHALE: squeeze the abdomen inwards and try to let the air out of the lungs in incremental bits whilst keeping the rib-cage lifted. You want to think about releasing the air from the top to the bottom of the lungs bit by bit. By doing this you will engage the muscles that will keep the torso in expansion for a beneficial amount of time. Try to breathe out for as long as you can. If you can breathe out to a count of eight or nine (or more if possible),

you will start to strengthen the muscles of the trunk.

Practise off-horse first. You may experience some slight light-headedness initially, but persevere and this should resolve as you rid the lungs of stale CO_2. Once you have done a few breaths on the ground, do it next time you are riding. Practise controlling your exhalation as you ask for a downward transition and see how it affects your horse.

TROUBLESHOOTING

If you have trouble getting the feeling of lifting and expanding your rib-cage, grab a strap or a bandage, or even a lead rope, and cross it around your waist. Keep a bit of tension in it and breathe in, into the strap. Maintain the tension in the strap for as long as possible as you breathe out.

Use a strap around your waist if you struggle to lift the rib-cage up and out. Keep some tension on the strap to help you find the intercostal muscles that will help you do this movement.

7 Mobilize

After aligning and expanding your body, the next pillar to moving well is mobilizing key areas that become restricted through daily life. Some of these movements involve adjustments to postures you will do already, and some can be added in to your day with minimal disruption. Mobilizing is essential but it does not have to be big, elaborate moves that make the change. Transformation can occur through small, regular and targeted movements. This chapter will introduce you to mobilizing moves for each segment of your body.

SHOULDER MOBILITY SEQUENCE

Keeping the shoulders mobile is crucial for enabling the shoulder girdle and arms to function as they should. Any restrictions in the shoulders are compensated for in the lower back, and when the shoulders are not mobile, the upper body and neck are forced into sitting in too much tension. This creates a postural drag to the muscles and can cause upper back pain, neck tension and headaches.

The following is an excellent sequence to do throughout the day. If you work at a desk you can do it from there, or take a minute out of your schedule and complete the sequence three times, as many times a day as you can!

1. Starting with your thumbs on your hips, stand with your feet hip width apart (you can do this sitting too). Keep the ribs above the hips and shoulders above your ribs.

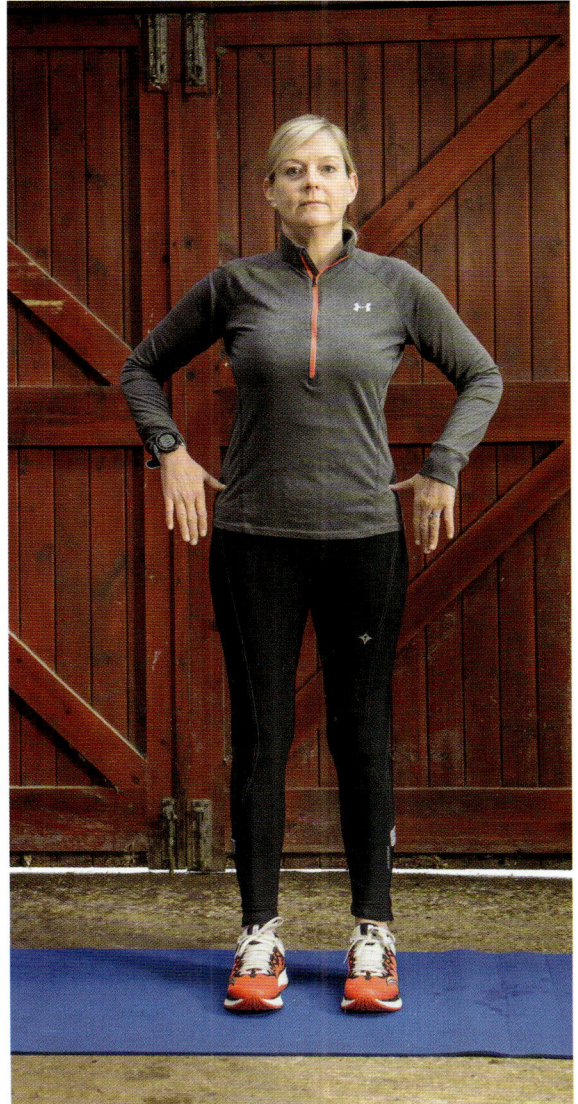

To start the shoulder mobility sequence, stand with your feet hip width apart, with your hips over your heels and your upper body in alignment, and place your thumbs on your hips.

2. Slide your thumbs up the side of your body to your armpits, keeping your elbows lifted.
3. Take the back of your hands to the back of your head.
4. Take both arms straight up overhead and finish the sequence by drawing a big circle with the arms and bringing them back down to your sides.

Repeat three times. If you have a seated job, aim to do this sequence every hour. It can also be really useful to do before you put the saddle on so that you release the shoulders before having to lift the saddle. This ensures that your lower back does not hyperextend for you to reach your horse's back.

Slide your thumbs up to your armpits, keeping the elbows lifted.

Take the back of your hands to the back of your head. Keep the ribs down.

RHOMBOID ROUSING

The thoracic region between the scapulae is vulnerable to immobility and inappropriate loading through poor positioning of the ribs, tight shoulders and a chin that moves away from the spine. Bringing mobility back to this area is incredibly useful for maintaining the health of the thoracic spine and its connection to the scapulae. It is also great for keeping the scapulae moving over the rib-cage, which is really useful for preparing the area for strengthening and for establishing a great anchor for your contact with the reins.

1. Beginning on all fours, keep your arms underneath your shoulders, your knees hip width apart and your back softly in neutral. For the duration of this movement your elbows stay straight. You are going to be moving the middle of your back, not your arms.

Reach your arms overhead and circle back down to the sides of your body to complete the sequence.

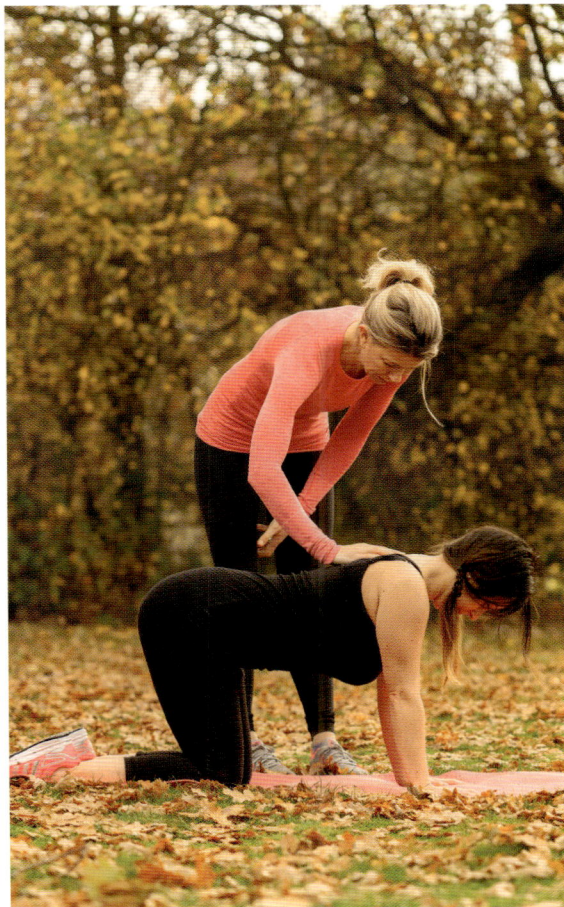

Get onto all fours, with your back in neutral, arms beneath shoulders and thighs horizontal.

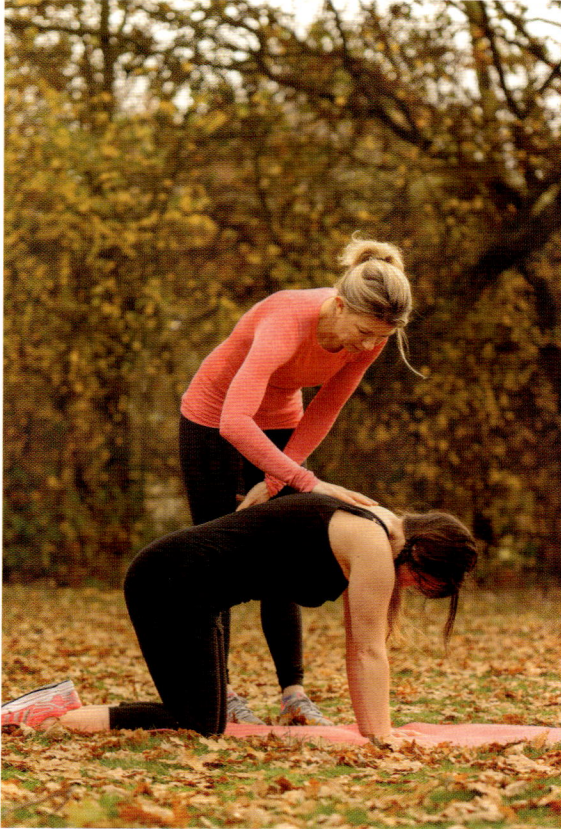

Push up between your shoulder blades and hold for 5–10 seconds.

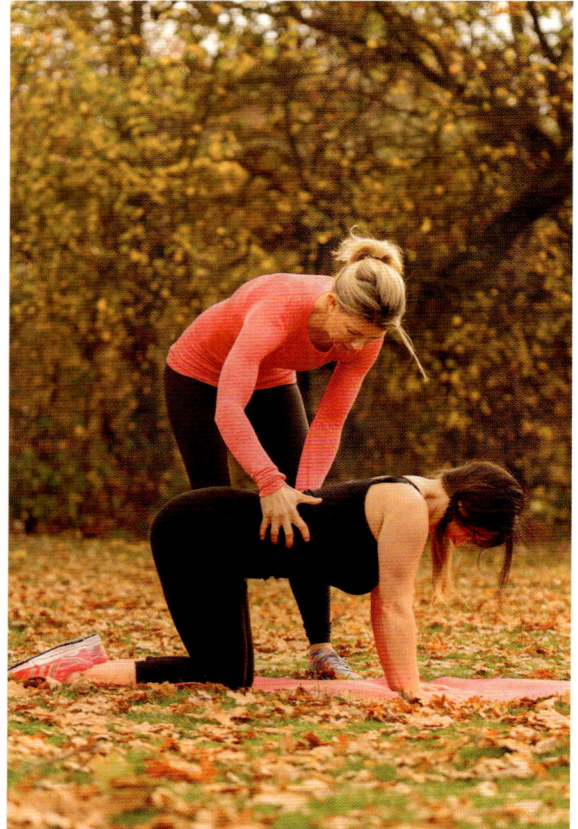

Let the middle of your back drop down between your shoulder blades whilst keeping your arms straight.

2. Push the middle of your back upwards, as if you were making space for a beach ball underneath your chest. Try not to raise the rest of your back; this is a targeted move just for the region between your scapulae. (If it is helpful, have someone place their hand in the right area and push up into it.)

3. Once you have pushed the back up, let it drop down between your shoulders, still keeping your elbows straight. You should have the feeling that you are bringing your scapulae towards each other.

Repeat fifteen to twenty times.

WINDMILL

Rotation of the mid-section of the back can be really neglected in everyday life, and this is to the detriment of your position and ability to be adaptable in the saddle. Waist and thoracic rotation is essential for a balanced position, and this move is great as it also moves the upper body independently from the pelvis – another key feature of an effective, balanced and secure seat.

Standing with a wide stance, hinge from the hips and take your left hand to touch your right foot, and then swap to take your right

Standing with a wide stance, reach up and take one arm down to the opposite foot. Raise the other arm straight up and follow the direction of the hand with your head. Repeat the other side.

hand to touch your left foot. Aim to keep your pelvis pointing straight ahead, keep the upward arm straight from the shoulder and turn your head gently to allow your gaze to follow the upward-reaching hand.

Repeat ten to fifteen times each side.

FORWARD BENDING

As you know, your hip joint can become stuck very easily through poor postural and movement habits. Bending forwards is a movement you will do quite often during the day. The way you do it can either improve the mobility of your hips and strengthen your glutes, or add to the wear and tear on your lower back.

1. Most people tend to bend forward by curling their spine, as shown in the photo.

This posture flexes the lower back, which brings the vertebrae closer together and presses onto the discs.
2. Instead the hips should be the hinge for the body, its fulcrum; as such, bending forward gives you a great opportunity to keep mobility in the hip joint, stretch the hamstrings and strengthen the glutes, whilst keeping the lower back lengthened and decompressed.

Stand with your feet hip width apart and push your pelvis back over your hips. Bring your upper body towards the ground whilst keeping your lower back flat. You may well feel a stretch down the back of your legs. It is likely that you will be able to reach closer to the ground with your hands. When you come to stand up again, squeeze your glutes together to raise your upper body.

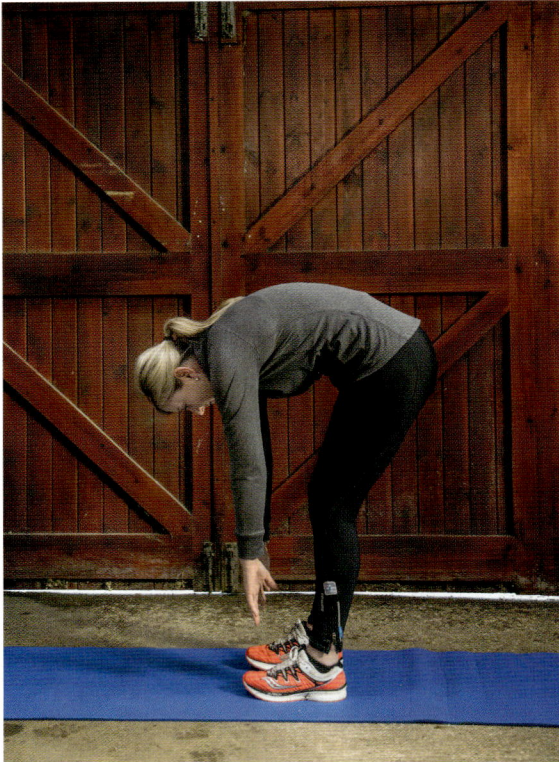

Forward bending using the lumbar spine puts it into flexion, weakening it and making it vulnerable to disc injury.

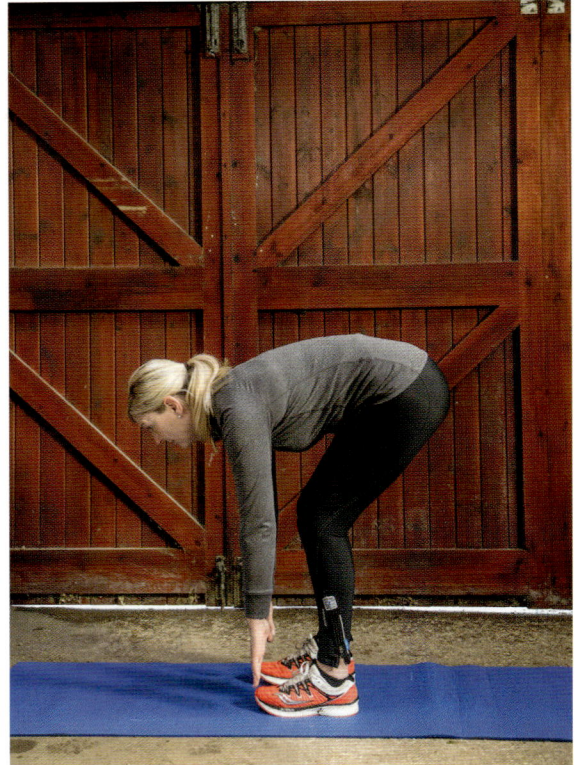

Correct bending is done by keeping the spine in neutral and hinging from the hips.

You can practise this movement for all sorts of jobs. Picking out your horse's feet is an excellent opportunity, particularly if you normally suffer with lower back pain from doing anything in this position.

Try to use this technique any time you need to bend forward. It really does make a difference to the mobility of your hips and the health of your lower back.

SUNRISE HAMSTRING STRETCH

This stretch is included here as it is very useful for the correct function of your hips and pelvis. It helps to keep the hamstrings lengthened and healthy, and, if you do the whole sequence of

taking the leg in an arc, you will also stretch the outside of the thigh and the adductors on the inside.

Start on your back (bolster your ribs if you need to, to keep them down and aligned), with knees bent or legs straight. Loop a resistance band/strap/bandage around the toes of one foot and gently extend the leg into the air. The aim is to keep the leg as straight as possible, so if this means it has to stay lower, that is fine. Apply a bit of pressure to the strap to gently bring your toes upwards so that your foot stays flat.

Take your leg out to the side, supporting the weight of it through the strap. You should feel a stretch on the inside of your leg. Try to keep your pelvis level on the floor.

Hamstring stretches are excellent to do at the end of the day. Use a strap and gently pull the toes towards your nose. Keep the leg as straight as possible.

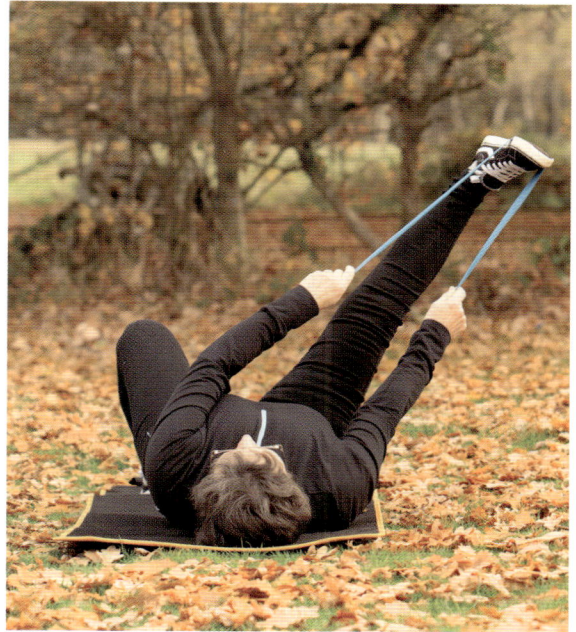

Take the leg out to the side, supporting the weight with the strap. This stretches the inside of the leg.

Take the leg across your body to stretch the outside of the thigh.

If your hamstrings are tight, use a bolster underneath your pelvis to apply some stretch without causing too much tension.

Next, gently bring the leg back to the centre before taking it across your body to stretch the outside of the thigh. Take your time, as this can be very tight. Try to keep the foot flat and just take the leg to the point of bind (where the stretch is quite strong but not uncomfortable).

If you have tight hamstrings, lifting the leg into this kind of stretch can make the muscles of the front of the leg contract and become tight. This will inhibit the quality of stretch you can achieve, so to improve the stretch in this situation, bolster your pelvis by placing a pillow or cushion or bolster underneath it. This helps to lessen the angle that the pelvis is sitting at, which helps to reduce the tension at the front of the leg when you want to target the hamstrings.

Hold each stretching position for twenty to twenty-five seconds.

SHOULDER FLOOR SWEEP

This is an incredibly effective exercise for improving both shoulder mobility and the relationship of the three parts of the shoulder girdle. The shoulder joints have to rotate and the scapulae have to move over the ribs, and it is all done from having the thoracic spine in the right place, so you are really targeting the muscles responsible for attaching the scapulae to the thoracic spine.

Lying on your back, with legs either bent or straight, bolster your ribs and shoulders if necessary (see Chapter 5). Take your arms out to the side and turn your palms upwards, touching your thumbs to the floor. Gently move your arms (keeping them as straight as possible) up towards the top of your head, keeping your thumbs and your elbows in contact with the floor.

Go slowly and do not worry if you cannot get very far without your elbows or your thumbs wanting to lift off the ground. Go as far as you can with them still touching the floor and stay in that position whilst taking two or three deep breaths. Try to revisit this exercise each day.

a) Lying on your back, with a bolster if you need one, take your arms out to the sides with your thumbs on the floor. b) Slide your thumbs up towards the top of your head, keeping the forearm and elbow on the floor. Only go as far as you can whilst your arm is on the floor.

LEGS ON THE WALL

This is an adductor stretch (for the muscles on the inside of your thigh), but it is also an excellent relaxation pose.

Find a clear wall and sit sideways next to it, with your pelvis quite close to the wall. Swivel around and put your legs up onto the wall. Slowly stretch your legs out to the side. You should feel a stretch on the inside of your legs. Settle here for as long as you like! The adductors can get really tight from riding, so this is a great way to keep them healthy and ensures that they are not negatively affecting the position of your hip joint.

This adductor stretch is also excellent for relaxation. Let your legs move outwards as they loosen with the stretch.

PSOAS RELEASE/PELVIC RESET

The psoas muscle affects the position of your lumbar spine and when it is tight it can pull your pelvis into a posterior tilt. However, it can still sit in a shortened position if your pelvis tips forward, and if you sit for any amount of time in daily life, the chances are this muscle needs a bit of attention. You will need a yoga block or a stack of books for this movement.

A tight psoas muscle can pull the pelvis out of alignment. Using a block or a cushion, place it under the lower part of your pelvis and allow gravity to pull the top of your pelvis down to the floor.

Lying on your back, bend your knees and place the block under the lower part of your pelvis, just above the top of your hamstrings. Let gravity lower the top of your pelvis and your lower back to the floor; do not use any muscular activity to force your body into any position. The tensile loading that gravity will apply to the pelvis in this position is enough to help stretch the psoas muscle. You may not feel very much, or you might feel a pull on one side more than the other, or you might feel the same amount on both sides. This is a really useful release, so stay here for a few minutes; even if you do not feel a huge stretch, it will be making a difference!

Separating the hip joint from the pelvis is essential for a good seat. Slowly slide your leg out to the side of your body. You can start with a bent knee, and progress to having a straight leg as shown here. Please note, do not do this if you have a hip replacement.

FREE THE HIPS

This is a movement that helps to improve how the hips move in general, and specifically to improve their ability to move independently from the pelvis which, as you have seen, is essential to a good seat in the saddle and an effective leg position.

Lying on your front, support your head on your hands and slowly bend one knee and bring the leg up and out to the side of your body, keeping the knee on the floor. You can start with the leg in this bent position and progress to a straight leg as you feel able. Settle into this stretch for thirty seconds or more and repeat on the other side.

Author's note: do NOT do this stretch if you have an artificial hip.

SQUATTING

Being able to get into a full squat is a movement that the body is born to do, yet with years of accumulating hip stiffness, ankle and calf tension and pelvic immobility through lack of use, it is a movement that is completely forgotten. The benefits of being able to squat are outlined in Chapter 2, but it is a fantastic movement for ankle, hip and pelvic health. It not only mobilizes but also strengthens the muscles of the pelvis. As it is likely not a move that you do, getting into a full squat is not going to happen immediately. The secret is to take steps to build up to it, so here is your squat preparation sequence.

Stage 1. The mobility of your hips is critical for being able to get into a full squat, and it is likely that they are not going to be as mobile as they could be. Start on all fours, hands underneath your shoulders and your spine in neutral. You are going to slowly lower your bottom to your heels whilst keeping the back in neutral. As soon as your pelvis wants to tuck under, you have reached the range of hip mobility that you currently have. Tucking under is the body's way of offloading the lack of mobility at the hip joint to the lower back – something that you do not want to happen. Lowering yourself slowly, you will feel when your pelvis wants to tuck. If not, line yourself up in front of a mirror so you can check.

In photos a and b, the pelvis and spine are still in neutral. In photo c the pelvis has started to tuck. When you have reached the end of your hips' mobility, come up slightly to make

sure that the pelvis is in neutral and stay in that position for about thirty seconds. If you do this every day, you will improve how well your hips can move. You are aiming to get

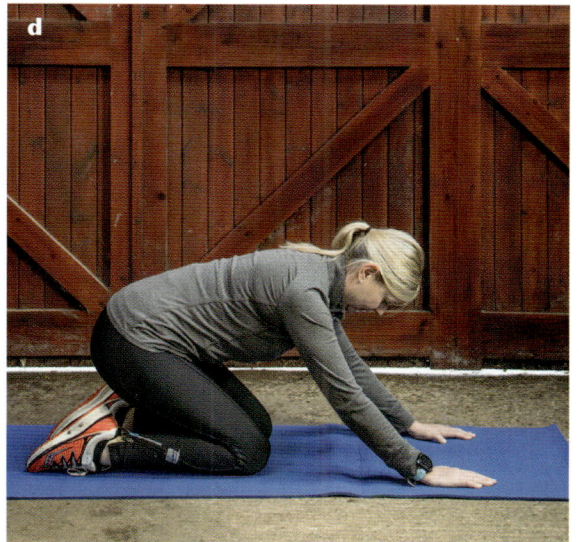

a) On all fours, make sure your hips are over your knees and your hands are underneath your shoulders. Keep the neutral curve in your spine, making sure the tailbone is lifted slightly. b) and c) Lower the pelvis down towards the heels whilst keeping the pelvis in neutral. d) As soon as it starts to tuck underneath, you have reached the end of your hips' mobility. Stay in this zone and let the hips receive some new load. Keep practising until you can get all the way to your heels.

The next stage of deep squat preparation is to use a towel or bolster underneath your heels until you get enough ankle flexibility not to need one.

A full, deep squat.

your bottom to your heels without tucking the pelvis under before you move on to the next stage.

Stage 2. Bolstered heels and squat with support
The next stage is to get into position but with a bolster or rolled-up towel underneath your heels so you can start to put the weight into the back of your body (the glutes), which will start to build strength. This stage will be supported by doing your calf/ankle stretches as well, as it will increase the flexibility of your ankles and the length of your calf muscles.

You might also need to support yourself in the squat by holding on to a chair or table leg, and that is fine. Your body will benefit from the movement, but at this stage you might not have the strength in your glutes or back to hold it without support.
Try to do some form of squat practice each day. Your entire body will thank you.

Stage 3. Full squat
This is the aim for all of your squat preparations. To be able to sit into a full squat will tone and strengthen your pelvic floor muscles, mobilize the hips and ankles, and help

Using a chair, table or counter, place your hands on it and walk your legs back. Hinge from the hips and sink down into the upper body stretch.

to strengthen the glutes, lower back and entire pelvic girdle. It is an excellent posture to get into for an improved seat in the saddle.

THORACIC STRETCH

Reaching the top of the spine by yourself can be really difficult, but quite often it can feel really tight and immobile. This is an easy stretch to do, as long as you have something to hold on to.

Find a chair, table or counter top and hold onto it. Move your feet backwards and place them quite far apart. Hinge forward from the hips, and lower your upper body until you feel the stretch across the top of your back.

8 Strengthen

Strengthening the body is only beneficial if you are strengthening the right things, in the right places. That means your body must be aligned, with key areas able to move (as you learnt in Chapter 7). Strength comes from muscles that are able to contract and relax, and this comes from muscles working in harmony and balance with each other. This is achieved through the mobilizing movements you have learnt, and the alignment protocols that are so important. Remember, the aim is to strengthen from a place of alignment, so that you are improving the right things rather than strengthening a dysfunction.

The following strengthening movements focus on the back of the body and the hips. There are no abdominal exercises apart from help for diastasis recti issues, which is a movement that can be used for general abdominal health even if you have no separation. The general message, if you want to continue doing exercises for the front of your body, is to change the ratio. For every abdominal exercise you do, you should do three times as much for your back. As long as you make strengthening the back a priority, you can do some abdominal work without concern.

large, more superficial muscles (the ones that can so often go into spasm) to release, allowing controlled movement and moving you away from pain. This posture is included in your daily plan (*see* Chapter 9) as it is so powerful in removing and preventing lower back pain.

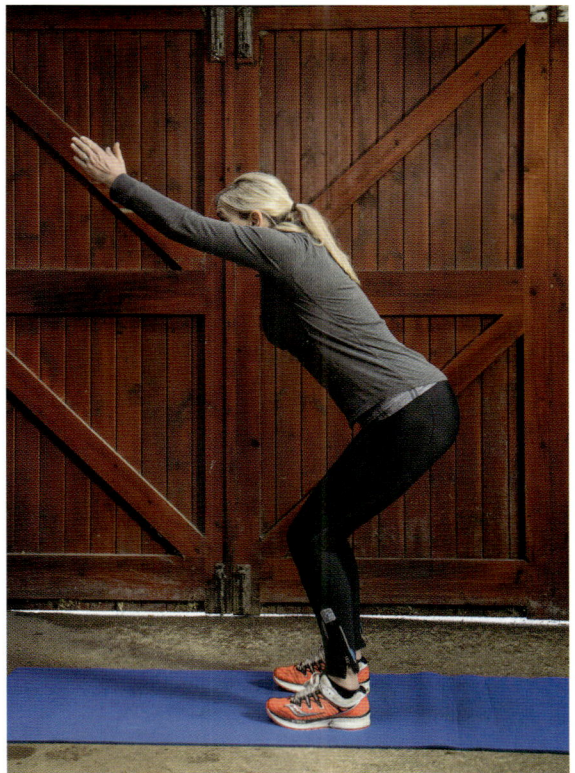

This modified chair pose is the best lower back strengthening exercise there is. Stand with feet at least hip-width apart, soften the knees and push your bottom out behind you. Hinge forward slightly from the hips and reach your hands up and press them together. Hold for three expansion breaths.

MODIFIED CHAIR POSE

This posture is similar to the chair pose in yoga (but with some differences) and it is excellent for lower back strength. It fires up the deep vertebral stabilizers (multifidi), bringing strength at the deepest level. This allows the

Stand with your feet hip-width apart with soft knees. Back your hips up so that your pelvis is over your heels. Hinge from the hips and imagine you are going to drop down into a chair behind you. Bring your arms either side of your head and press your fingers together. Keep the back in neutral. You should feel the lower back, so do not be alarmed if your attention is focusing on the feeling here; this is a good sign! Stay in this posture for three expansion breaths. Squeeze your glutes to bring your upper body back to upright.

Do this posture twice a day. It is safe even if you do have back pain as it decompresses the lower back and strengthens/stabilizes it, which is essential for reducing pain.

BACK EXTENSIONS

These are excellent for strengthening the complete posterior chain, targeting the glutes, hamstrings, lower and upper back.

Lying on your front, support your head on your hands. With your feet together, squeeze your glutes and lift your legs off the ground.

This is not about the height; be sure not to overextend your back to get your legs off the floor. The point of this exercise is to strengthen the back of the legs and the lower back, so form, as always, is more important than distance or height. Lift the legs and hold for thirty to fifty seconds.

Once you are happy with this, you can add in the upper body lift as well. Keeping the arms bent and the hands underneath your head, lift the upper body and the legs at the same time. Hold this position for thirty to sixty seconds and repeat three to five times.

STRENGTHENING SQUAT

This is a different squat from the one you learnt in Chapter 7. This one is more akin to the type you would do in the gym, but with a few essential form pointers. The point of the squat is to strengthen the glutes and hamstrings at the back of the body, with a bit of quadricep work at the front of the thigh too. It is a great exercise for riders as, when done correctly, it strengthens and mobilizes

Back extensions help to build strength for the whole spine. You can lift the upper body or the legs, or both at the same time. Squeeze your glutes to lift the legs and keep your gaze low.

the soft tissues of the hips and pelvis, builds strength in the all-important glutes and can really build great postural control in the saddle, particularly for rising trot and for correct jumping position.

Standing with your feet hip-width apart, lower your bottom down as if you were going to sit in a chair behind you. The secret to a really beneficial squat, rather than one that can cause some wear and tear, is to keep

a) and b) Squats are excellent for strengthening the glutes and back. Stand with feet hip-width apart and imagine you are going to sit in a chair behind you. Keep your shins vertical. Come up to standing by squeezing the glutes and repeat.

your shins vertical and your knees above your ankles. Most squats done in the gym see the knees coming over the big toe. This overloads the front of the leg and subsequently puts too much pressure on the knee joint. You want this movement to strengthen the back of your body and mobilize your hips so vertical shins are essential.

Repeat fifteen to twenty times, three times a day.

BRIDGES

These are an excellent exercise for glute strength and lateral hip strength.

Lying on your back with your knees bent and your feet hip-width apart, squeeze your glutes and lift your pelvis off the floor. You are aiming for a straight line from your chest through your pelvis to your knees.

Hold for thirty to sixty seconds. When you lower, be sure that your pelvis reaches the ground first so that you do not tilt or change the position of your spine.

ONE-LEGGED BRIDGES

This takes the previous exercise a step further. You are now strengthening the lateral hip muscles whilst stabilizing the body as you lift the other leg off the ground.

In the same position as for the bridge exercise, from here lift one foot off the ground and extend the leg, keeping it in line with the height of the knee.

SIDE-STEPPING WITH STRAP

Weak lateral hip muscles can be the cause of many hip, knee and foot problems that affect you both on the ground and in the saddle.

Use this bridge exercise for glute and leg strength. Make sure the hips come up in line with the knees. Lower the pelvis back to the ground, keeping it in neutral.

An advanced version of the bridge to challenge lateral strength. Lift one leg off the floor and straighten it, keeping the knee in line.

This is an excellent way of bringing strength to these muscles. You will need a strap or resistance band.

Standing with feet hip-width apart, step into the band and keep it tight. Take a step to the side with one leg, following with the other leg, whilst keeping the tension in the band throughout the movement. Take five steps one way, then return the other way five steps, and repeat the whole exercise three times. You will need to hinge slightly forward from the hips, keeping them over your heels.

Lateral hip strength is critical for a successful leg position in the saddle. Use a strap to side-step with resistance. Take five steps one way, and then return back to where you started.

a) The hip hike is excellent for pelvic and hip strength and also for firing up the multifidi of the lower spine. Press the standing leg into the ground to raise the other leg slightly off the floor. Keep the upper body stacked over the pelvis. b) Use a block to increase the amount of pelvic and hip mobility required, and increase the strength required on the outside of the hip to stabilize you.

HIP HIKES

As it is so important to strengthen the muscles of the hips, this is another targeted exercise that also helps the lower back. To start with, you can do this exercise without a block, but as you become stronger and more mobile, doing it from a block will increase its effectiveness.

Standing with your feet hip-width apart and your pelvis over your heels, press one leg down into the ground to lift the other leg slightly off the floor. It is important that you are thinking about pressing the standing leg further into the floor as opposed to lifting the other leg up, because you will then use your lower back and not activate the muscles of the hip.

The leg stays straight, so there is no bending of your knees.

Make sure you do not lean your hip out to one side to lower your leg (see photo). The drop from the block requires more pelvic mobility so if you cannot do it without leaning to one side and pushing your hip out, stay and practise for longer on the ground.

a) Carrying heavy items can create too much drag on your shoulder joint, stretching the ligaments. b) Make sure you support the joint using the muscles of your upper arm to counteract the drag of what you are carrying by lifting the upper arm towards the shoulder joint.

CARRYING

Carrying is something riders do a lot of, particularly looking after horses. Water buckets, haynets, saddles and wheelbarrows are constantly adding loads to your body that can either help to strengthen it or can cause some problems. Carrying is an excellent way to strengthen the body, and carrying things in different ways is certainly encouraged. There are some techniques that can help you make sure it is serving your body in the best way.

Water buckets: carrying anything heavy on the end of straight arms has the potential to load the ligaments of the shoulder joint rather than the muscles, which are the structures that actually have the strength and elasticity to cope with loads. All too often, carrying heavy items exerts so much pull on the arm that the ball of the shoulder joint is moved slightly away from the socket. The ligaments are loaded and become lax; once they are lax they cannot go back, which weakens and reduces the integrity of the shoulder joint and can make it vulnerable

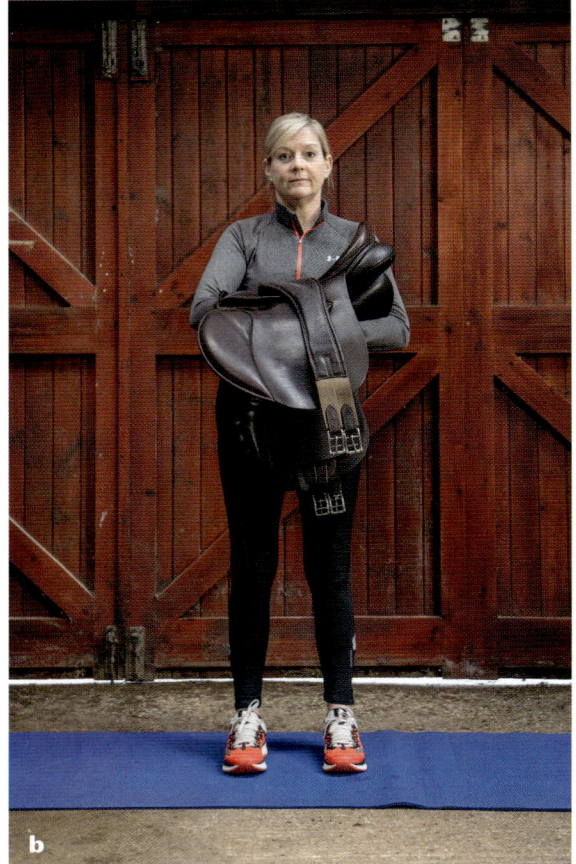

a) and b) Change the way you carry everyday items, like your saddle, to load different parts of your body.

to issues such as frozen shoulder and subluxation.

Instead of carrying from your ligaments, support the joint with the muscles of your arm and shoulder by keeping the shoulder joint in position. This is a subtle move of activating the muscles of the top of your arm as if you were lifting the shoulder up.

In the photo you can see how the shoulder has been pulled down and the body taken out of alignment. In the next photo the shoulder has been stabilized by an upward activation of the arm muscles and the body can stay in alignment, and the shoulder joint is being strengthened.

Try to carry items like your saddle in different ways, so that more of your body is loaded. Be mindful of being aligned as you do.

ROLLOVER

This is a lovely exercise to do for anybody suffering with separation of the abdominals (*see* Chapter 3), and it is a great way of helping the front of the body stay strong without creating any negative effects on the back, whether your abdominals are together or apart. For this exercise you will need something that weighs between 2 and 5kg, depending on what feels comfortable. The aim is to not have to strain or move your body in order to move the weight through the complete arc.

Lying on your back with your legs straight, hold the weight in your hands at your belly. Very slowly, with straight arms, lift the weight up and over your head to come to rest on the ground above your head. Then lift the weight up and slowly bring it back down the arc to where it started. You should feel the front of your body doing some work. Repeat this exercise twelve to fifteen times and adjust the weight as necessary.

a), b), c) and d) An excellent, low-force way of strengthening the front of the body. Holding some weight in your hands, lift it up and over your head and then return to your starting position and repeat. Go slowly and you will feel the front of your body activate.

9 A Day in the Life

By now you are making progress through your movement story and can soon start to implement what you have learnt into your everyday life. You have discovered how your movement habits might be affecting you, you have exercises to help you start to unravel and change the shape of your body, and now it is time to find out how to implement this into your normal life. The aim of all this information is not to burden you with more things on your 'to do' list. It is designed to be incorporated into your daily life whilst building awareness and starting to change your movement habits.

This chapter will explore some of the key movements you can do alongside your normal activities, which will kick start your movement journey in the easiest, most user-friendly way. The postures/movements that are included are the ones that can make the biggest difference to you straight away, establishing a foundation onto which you can stack the rest of the movement protocols.

It is, of course, simply a guide and it can be tailored to what suits you as you become more and more familiar with what your body needs.

FIRST THINGS FIRST

Your morning routine is a great way to get some positive movement into your body. Use the modified chair pose as you clean your teeth to strengthen your lower back and to make those minutes at the sink count even more. If you have a sore lower back, or you want to avoid a sore lower back, this is the posture for you! It will fire up those deep spinal stabilizing muscles and start building a healthy, strong core that you can take into the saddle with you. If you suffer from pain in your lower back, doing this pose twice a day for two weeks can significantly reduce your pain levels.

THE MOVING MANTRA

Alignment

Moving from a place of alignment is the golden rule for building a stronger, more

Check your alignment! Are you standing or walking with one foot pointing outwards?

mobile and pain-free body. Start building awareness of how you are moving into your everyday life: how do you walk down the stairs? where is your upper body as you walk the dog? how are you standing when you are talking to somebody?

The checklist for alignment is:

- stand with your feet hip-width apart
- back your pelvis up so your hips are over your heels
- drop your bottom rib so it is sitting in line with the top of your pelvis
- drop your shoulders so they are in line with your ribs

- gently pull the base of your head upwards, bringing the chin back towards the spine
- when walking upstairs or uphill, keep the shins vertical and the knees over the heels, with your shoulders over your hips
- when walking downstairs or downhill, allow your hip to drop down to the next step so you can keep the rest of your body in alignment

This is a movement practice that you really can use throughout the day without having to take time out. It is incredibly valuable to the way your body is going to function both in and out of the saddle. As well as building the right muscles in the body,

a) Use your hips as a hinge for everyday activities like picking out feet so that you use these tasks to build mobility into your body, and not stress your lower back as in b).

practising moving in alignment will also build the body awareness that is so critical to good riding.

HINGE, DON'T HUNCH

Bending forwards is a movement you will do many times throughout your day, probably without realizing just how often you do it. Done correctly, it provides a fantastic opportunity to get some valuable movement moments into your hips and hamstrings, instead of stressing your spine.

You saw in Chapter 7 how to bend forward correctly, and this applies to every single move that requires your upper body to get lower to the floor. The hips are the hinge of the body, so bend from the hips whilst keeping your back as flat as possible. This ensures that you are improving the overall mobility of the hips, giving the hamstrings a nice little stretch and saving your lumbar spine from unnecessary wear and tear and potential muscle spasms.

Use this technique for picking out feet, poo picking, picking things up off the floor, getting into a low cupboard or eyeballing the dog.

THE SHOULDER SAVIOUR

Keeping the shoulder joints mobile is critical if the upper body is going to remain strong and in a good posture. It is especially important if you want to avoid stressing your lower back when tacking up, and to be able to achieve a consistent contact when you ride. Having shoulders that can move is crucial to the overall success of your biomechanics, and this shoulder mobility sequence (which you learnt in Chapter 7) can be done at your desk as often as you like during the day. Aim for three repetitions every hour. It is also really useful to do before you ride and when you wake up. Even if you do not work at a desk, do it anyway!

ALL ABOUT THE BASE

Your feet are the unsung heroes of your body and can cause a multitude of issues from being weakened inside shoes. Where possible, try to incorporate some barefoot time around the home and add in a few stretches as you go. Rolling your foot on a tennis or golf ball is also a great way of relieving tension in the sole of the foot.

FLOOR SITTING AND NO HANDS

You have seen how sitting in a chair impacts the shape of your body, and how this is carried over into how well you are able to sit in the saddle, so the next activity to implement into your daily schedule is to sit on the floor rather than the couch when you are at home. Sitting on the floor makes you use more of your body, which means you are using more cells, which means you are keeping more cells healthy. Floor sitting is also not as comfortable as sitting on the couch so you will move into different positions more often. This is an excellent way of getting more micro movement into your body and to target areas that may have been neglected throughout the day.

Interestingly, it has been suggested that your ability to sit down and stand up without using your hands is an indicator of increased life expectancy as it is used as a parameter for general health. You can start practising this when you go to sit in a chair and stand up again. Try to do the movement without using your hands, and aim to progress to floor sitting and standing up just by using your legs. This is an excellent exercise to practise, whatever stage or shape your body is in. Go slowly, and bit by bit you will improve your strength on a micro level, which will help you perform this macro, whole body movement.

SQUATTING

In Chapter 8 you learned how to build up to being able to get into a full squat. This is included in your daily movement guide because it is such an important, functional move for your hips and pelvis, whose health is *critical* to riding success. Try to take a few minutes each day to do stage one of squat prep and see where the journey takes you.

CONSCIOUS CARRYING

The shape of your body is determined by your alignment, and alignment is so important because of the loads the body has to carry. This is not so much about weight, but about *how* the body carries the weight (of the body itself and anything external that you need to move from one place to another). Carrying things differently during the day will use different structures and therefore cells, which means you are giving more movement to more of your body. This is always the aim for the success of the human biomechanical system. So lift your bag differently, avoid using a basket at the supermarket and hold things in your arms, carry the saddle in a different position and get creative on anything else that you can think of. All of these things, although they seem tiny and insignificant, can really help the body develop more overall strength and balance between used and unused cells, which means there is less of an imbalance between muscle strength and weakness.

Stretching the fingers is a really useful and easy way of reducing the amount of tension through your arms and hands, helping to improve shoulder mobility and the elasticity of muscles, which is helpful for your contact on the reins.

HANDS AND FOREARMS

Applying stretch to the fingers each day can be a really useful way of stretching out the muscles of the forearms, which can contribute to shoulder tension. Try stretching each finger for ten to twelve seconds each day.

   Bringing the backs of your hands together is a great stretch for the muscles of the forearms. See how much tension you are carrying in your arms by how difficult it is to get into this position!

Bringing the backs of the hands together stretches the forearms and improves wrist mobility.

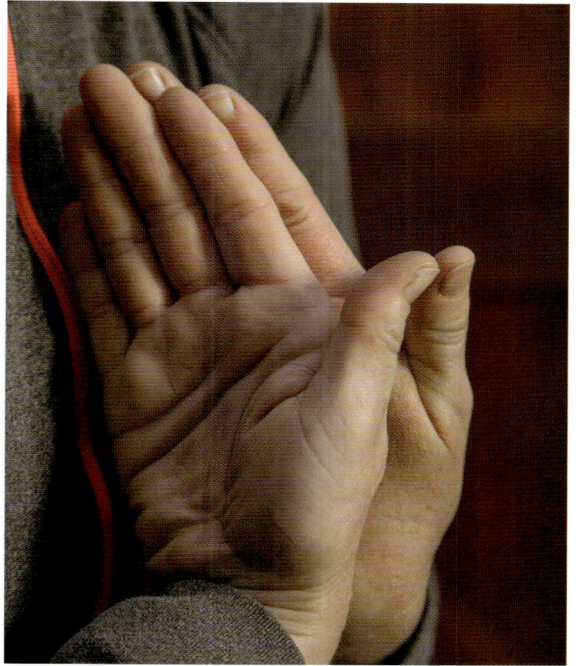

10 You Ride How You Move

Owning a horse, learning how to ride it and then learning how to train it is a journey that is as exciting as it is challenging, rewarding as it is devastating, and as time-consuming as any addiction. The success of any horse/rider relationship lies in the detail – the detail of how the horse is managed and how it is ridden. Competition relies on detail; in dressage particularly, the positioning of the horse's body is scrutinized at every moment. Successful jumping relies on the detail of getting to the fence, over it and away from it in a way that keeps the horse safe, balanced and clear of contact. The difference between success and failure can be mere millimetres – it all comes down to the detail.

It is through the detail that the farrier can either enhance how the horse moves or make his life really difficult; it is in the detail of fitting a saddle that can improve or wreck how the horse and rider can interact with each other, how the horse can move and how the rider can sit. It is through the detail of feeding and stable management that your horse can thrive or be in a state of health that limits how he can perform. The same is true for your own body. This book has taken you on a journey of details, focusing on the small, micro pieces of information that often get overlooked. But even if they appear trivial or unnecessary, it is in the detail that true transformations can be made.

Your body is a collection of details that more often than not get clumped together and ignored because the desire to complete larger, macro movements or accomplish some task that looks impressive outweighs the attention needed to really make sure the system is working as well as it can. The desire for short-term 'success' or apparent immediate change blurs and clouds the path to true mastery of your body, and quite often that of your horse.

As a rule, riders try really hard to create the best environment for their horse both in and out of the arena, but what if riding wasn't about trying harder? What if it was about learning to use the system that you already have? You can try as hard as you like in a faulty system, and the results can only ever be, at best, mediocre. These chapters have explored the mechanics of your body, and how your body is designed to move. You have seen how your movement habits and your environment shape your body and interrupt how it wants to be positioned, affecting not just your experience of your body on the ground, but also how your horse will experience it too.

The great news is that your body's correct operating system is still there, waiting for you to switch it on. It may be a bit rusty, but with a bit of elbow grease you can begin to unearth a well-oiled machine.

THE SEEDS OF TRANSFORMATION

A plant cannot grow without a seed. However hard you try, however much water or sunlight you give it, without the core or seed for growth, nothing is going to happen. You too might have the best horse and instructor and team and gear but without the seed of learning how to bring the best body to the saddle, your growth is going to be limited.

Moving in alignment, out of pain and with a strong core, still might not take you to the Olympics, but what it will do is cut out an awful lot of noise for you and your horse. If you have ever been to a crowded venue and tried to chat over loud music and other people shouting, you will know that communication with lots of background noise is unsatisfactory. Riding in a body that cannot sit comfortably with the horse, that aches and grips and bounces and kicks and fiddles, is creating a lot of background noise. If you can improve the signal, even a little bit, by reducing the static, your riding journey is able to move forward in the right way.

Riding better is always the priority for riders, just as improving at their sport is the priority for any athlete, but where hours of dedication go into preparing the swimmer's body, or the gymnast's or the ballerina's, the horse rider generally takes the body they have and puts it in the saddle, hoping their abilities will improve through riding practice. The problem is, the ability you improve through your riding practice is the way in which you are riding. If you consistently ride crookedly, you will practise riding crookedly. If you consistently ride with an elbow poking out, you will practise riding with an elbow poking out and will probably become very good at it! The aim should always be to become sufficiently body aware that you can correct problems as you go through your riding practice, but this awareness is only possible if you are mindful about how you are moving through the day. Most amateur riders do not have time to dedicate hours in the gym being supervised by a professional, and the whole point of this book was to show you that you do not need this to change how you show up in the saddle. It comes back to the detail: the detail of the movements you are making during the day and the way in which you are doing them. Little by little, step by step, you can transform the way you use your body just by strengthening your back, sitting on the floor a bit more and walking in alignment. I do not expect you to get as excited about the details of biomechanics as I do, but I would love you to get excited about the thought that you have power over how your body is going to feel, that you have ownership of how much pain you are going to be in, how mobile you are going to be and how balanced you can be in the saddle. The guidelines in this book are designed to give you the tools you need to enrich the quality of your life, because living in a body in pain is not a destination of choice for anyone.

Riders are asymmetrical and horses are asymmetrical so this is not about being perfectly even, but it is about improving what you have and being aware of what you are doing. The ABC of rider improvement is: Awareness Before Change. If you can be aware of your own asymmetries on the ground and take steps to improve how you move off-horse, you will have a much better chance of minimizing the effect of this asymmetry when you are in the saddle. Saddle fit is critical, and straightness training in your horse is essential, just as alignment of your own body is the foundation for everything else.

In summary, as a rider you are an athlete. Whether you have fitness support each day, or you do a class once a week, if you want to ride then you are an athlete. To keep things practical, because this is not about *pretending* to make a difference but actually *making* a difference, changing your movement habits during the day is the foundation for preparing your body to cope with what happens in the saddle and for minimizing the potentially damaging responses your horse might want to make for your crookedness. Most people's most basic movement patterns create lines of tension and asymmetries, lack of mobility, weakness and pain that only serve to build on an asymmetric base. If you pile weights or complex movement patterns on top of this unstable foundation, it will start to crumble. You have seen how to align, strengthen and mobilize your body just by changing how you walk, bend, sit and stand. You now understand the importance for strengthening the lower back, to guard it from pain and injury, and to improve your seat in the saddle, as well as avoiding giving your horse a sore back. A strong core and a lower back free from pain are crucial to any rider's success, and for allowing the horse to move as comfortably as possible. My hope is that you use this information in your daily life, to build the framework of your body into a strong, stable and aligned scaffolding onto which you can add extra 'fitness' or body awareness techniques. A class once a week from a body that has ingrained asymmetry and poor movement protocols will not do enough to change how you ride. It has to be a mindful, daily practice that will serve you in your life away from your horse as much as it will serve you when you are in the saddle.

The performance of both horse and rider is always a team effort, but getting your body into the best position it can be in is the most controllable aspect of your riding journey. Of course, we have seen that saddle interaction and horse asymmetry can and will influence your position in the saddle, and this is why it is critical to raise your awareness of where your body is in time and space so that you can recognize when something has gone awry. Working with a qualified saddle fitter, your coach, a physio and all members of your team is critical, whatever level of rider you are. If you ride a horse you have some responsibility for his welfare and comfort, and this is a team effort. What you can do on your own is start implementing what you have learnt in these pages, and it is my hope that you approach your body with a renewed interest and curiosity about how it can perform for you. It is my belief that we have been gifted a resource that is perfectly capable of transporting us through life in comfort, with strength and mobility to allow us to perform all the physical activities that we enjoy. This applies to riding too. It is an extraordinary sport that is unrivalled by any other in terms of complexity but it is also one of the most incredible sports to be a part of. I hope this information helps you move along your riding journey in a way that helps you and your horse enjoy every step you take.

Index

OTHER EQUESTRIAN TITLES FROM CROWOOD AND JA ALLEN

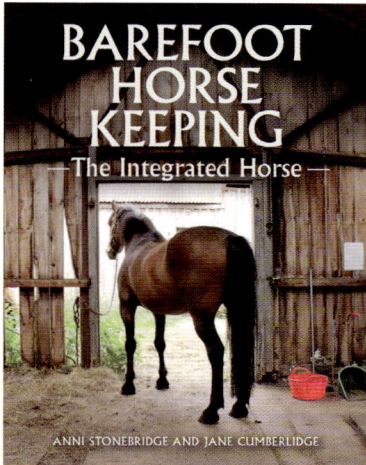

BAREFOOT HORSE KEEPING
— The Integrated Horse —
ANNI STONEBRIDGE AND JANE CUMBERLIDGE

978 1 78500 173 4

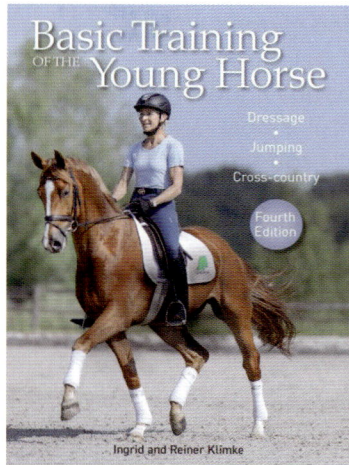

Basic Training OF THE Young Horse
Dressage • Jumping • Cross-country
Fourth Edition
Ingrid and Reiner Klimke

978 1 90880 988 9

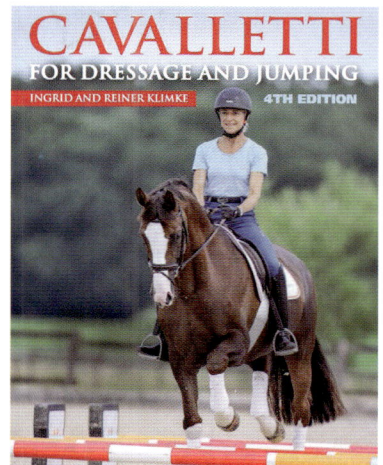

CAVALLETTI
FOR DRESSAGE AND JUMPING
INGRID AND REINER KLIMKE 4TH EDITION

978 1 90880 975 9

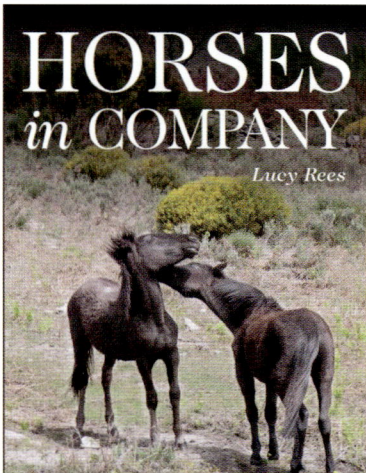

HORSES in COMPANY
Lucy Rees

978 1 90880 956 8

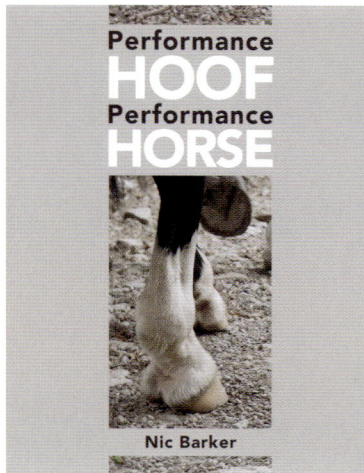

Performance HOOF Performance HORSE
Nic Barker

978 1 90880 970 4

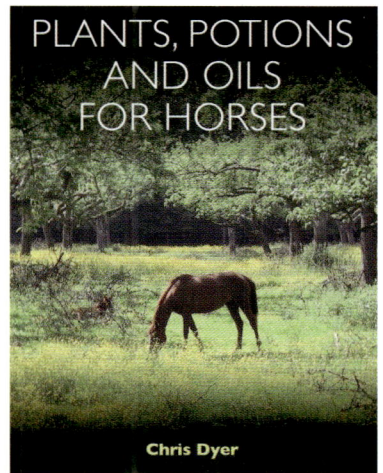

PLANTS, POTIONS AND OILS FOR HORSES
Chris Dyer

978 1 90880 958 2

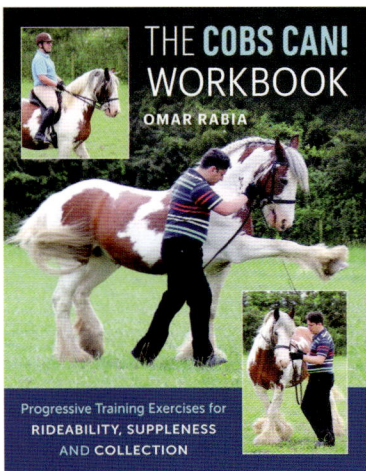

THE COBS CAN! WORKBOOK
OMAR RABIA
Progressive Training Exercises for
RIDEABILITY, SUPPLENESS AND COLLECTION

978 1 90880 930 8

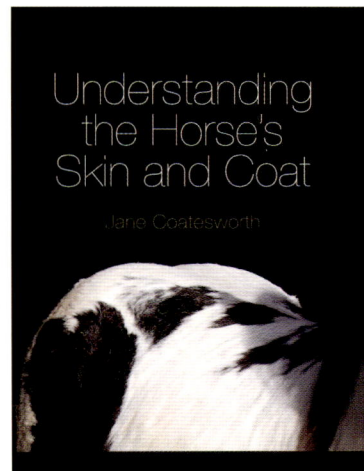

Understanding the Horse's Skin and Coat
Jane Coatesworth

978 1 90880 954 4

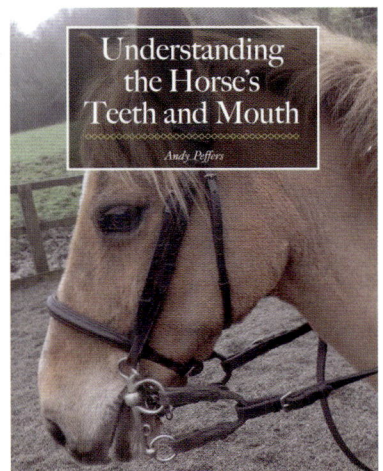

Understanding the Horse's Teeth and Mouth
Andy Peffers

978 1 90880 952 0